It's Just Head Hoo-Ha

It's Just Head Hoo-Ha
Overcome Anxiety using the PRISM Method

Junilda Wright

CONTENTS:

The PRISM Method	1
How to use this Book	5
What is Anxiety?	9
The Science Bit	13
Everything is just Energy	19
Your Emotional Vibration	21
PREPARE	27
C is for Current Story	31
R is for Replacement Story	39
E is for Emotional Engagement	46
A is for Achievement	48
T is for Triggers	50
E is for Envision	51
RELEASE & INVITE	57
Let go of what you don't want	61
Other People's Impact	67
Your Impact on Others	75
Your Timeline	79
Release the Negative	81
Invite the Good Stuff	87
New Neural Pathways	91
Visualisation	95
Sabotage	103

SHIFT 106
Plan 110
Manage Time 116
Interruption Techniques 119
Diaphragmatic Breathing 123
Self-Validation and Approval 126
Perfectionism 140
Catastrophic Thinking 147
Taking Action 150
Be Who You Want to Be 156
Bringing it all Together 158

MAINTAIN 165
Mindfulness & Meditation 167
Physical Exercise 171
Muscle Relaxation Technique 174
Gratitude 177
The Three Rs 179
Sleep 182
Your Safe Place 186
Food 189
Conclusion 192

Acknowledgments

You will notice I have used the pronoun 'we' throughout the book, even though there is only one name on the front cover. I have done this in full acknowledgment of the invaluable contribution my dear friend and Business partner, Jo Lang has made. Her pearls of wisdom and insight are woven into the book either as direct suggested additions or as a result of the hours of discussion we have had over the years, helping me shape the tools and techniques I have shared here.

I acknowledge Tanya Allen for all her love and support with editing this book. For her practical and considered feedback and for the nudges to keep going when it would have been all too easy to not finish and publish.

I acknowledge Audrey Lewis for the safe space she gives me every week to express my ideas, fears, and dreams so I can continue my own journey of self-discovery.

I acknowledge my amazing husband, Stu for believing in me and for listening to countless hours of my ramblings – or at least pretending to! And for coming up with the title for this amazing book.

And lastly, I acknowledge my friends and family for their words of encouragement and belief.

A heart-felt thank you to you all.

Foreword

We want to congratulate you on taking the brave move to do something about your anxiety. The biggest and most profound step to making a change in your life, is the decision to do something different.

Change can be challenging but change can also be a force for good - and we are here to prove it to you. Change happens all the time, often in unseen ways.

As you work through this book, we are going to help you identify what may have caused your anxiety - unlike modern medicine which rarely treats the root causes - so you don't just learn to cope with it, but overtime can leave it behind you.

We will show you in easy steps how to re-wire that beautiful big brain of yours to be on your side. We will help you identify where external factors such as school, culture and those around have had a negative impact - after all, we are social animals and the people and experiences in our life shape who we are -and how to gently shift away from the more negative influences.

Whatever your experience has been up to this point, you have the authority to change the way you respond going forward. Whether you can see it right now or not, you always have a choice.

Everything we know and do is a learned skill and within that truth, you can learn to be anything you want.

The first step in becoming the person you want to be is to make time for this transformation. Along the way you may be tempted to give up. Just know that if you do nothing, nothing happens.

So, as we guide you through this book, remember you are the one in control. Although we encourage you to take certain actions, you are doing this for yourself, and part of this journey will be helping you to see where you may self-sabotage and give you ways of adjusting that behaviour.

One of the worst ways we sabotage ourselves is thinking that we can't do something or that someone else needs to fix us. We are sold the idea in every Hollywood movie that to be happy, someone must save us. However, we believe that is utter rubbish and worse - something that will hold you in a pattern of victimhood throughout your life. So, within the pages of this book are all the techniques you need to step away from that mindset and become the glorious human you came here to be.

You will not be the same person on the other side of this process. If you fully embrace it, you will find your own true perception of life and the people within it. Your ability to control what happens in your life will shift. In most cases our clients tell us they no longer recognise the person they were when they began the journey - in the best possible way.

How far you take this transformation is always up to you. You are coming back to the real you, who was always there.

You ROCK!!

Disclaimer

The PRISM method is not meant to be a substitute for counselling or professional help but is designed to help you help yourself and support you through your journey to overcoming anxiety.

While the techniques we will share have been shown to have a positive effect, they are for guidance only, and you should take the advice of suitably qualified health professionals if you have any concerns about your emotional well-being or if negative thoughts are causing significant or persistent unhappiness.

Likewise, if you are taking any form of medication for your anxiety, please consult with your medical practitioner before making any decision to change or stop.

It's Just Head Hoo-Ha

The PRISM Method

It is safe to say we take, what some may call an unorthodox approach to helping our clients overcome anxiety. For us, it is all about restoring harmony.

Harmony is not a term used very much in everyday life. As you read the word harmony you may even think to yourself, 'that sounds a bit wishy-washy,' but harmony truly is the key to lasting happiness, positivity, peace, and self-confidence. It is something our society overlooks in the way we are taught to live our lives, yet this is where our individual power really lies.

When we talk about harmony we mean when your feelings, actions, ideas, and interests are in alignment with achieving inner peace and happiness. When you no longer feel like you are swimming upstream and that when you do encounter life's challenges, you are able to quickly and easily navigate through them to restore harmony again.

Nobody can create harmony for you; it comes from within. But when you achieve it, you find you are less at the mercy of other people to make you feel happy, to reassure you, to validate you. You can bounce back from negative life experiences. The external influences on you have less of an impact – people and their opinions, people sharing or withholding their love and support, the media telling you how to look and feel, what to eat and what to wear, where to go, what to do. You get to be in control, to trust yourself to make the choices that are right for you.

We guide you through this amazing process to help you find the right balance between doing what feels good for you and finding your place in the world.

The route back to harmony we will take you on will include a mix of cognitive, physical and spiritual techniques – all interwoven. We look at you as a whole person, not just the thoughts in your head.

No one single technique is truly effective on its own but bring them together and – BOOM! There will be huge shifts in the way you think and behave once you have worked your way through this book.

The world can feel like a scary place when you experience anxiety; full of doubt, fear and at times, overwhelm. Your anxiety reflects the way you are currently thinking. The way you are thinking is influencing the way you feel and the way you feel will dictate the way you behave, including the way your body may be physically responding. This is why we have some beef with the way we, as a society, use medication to overcome anxiety.

Although we agree there may be a need for medication as a short-term approach, for us, this is just treating the symptom and not the cause. Medication is designed to be a short-term help for a crisis, not an ongoing way of life. It is a sticking plaster on a serious wound. If you do not address 'why' you are thinking and feeling the way you are, things are not likely to change.

So, it will come as no surprise that we are going to delve deep into your thought patterns to help you to step out of your current mindset and to see things with a new perspective. Part of that journey is identifying where your fears stem from. What beliefs you are subconsciously holding that trigger these anxious thoughts and feelings.

It's Just Head Hoo-Ha

There are layers to this. There are your conscious thoughts that you are aware of – these are easy to identify and work with – and there are your subconscious thoughts. These are the big boys. They lurk beneath your awareness, influencing everything you feel, say, and do.

There are layers to your subconscious thoughts too. There are those that bob about just below the surface. These can often be brought to full awareness through talking therapies. But there are also those buried deep down. Thoughts that take some digging to identify, but with Reiki and Meditative techniques you can access and let go of. These tend to be the ones with the biggest influence on you.

This is truly where the magic happens and, for us, this is one of the aspects of our approach that sets our method apart.

We explore how your physical body is playing a part in your anxiety and how relaxation techniques are a powerful way to manage the symptoms. Relieving physical symptoms like headaches, muscle tension, and tightness in your chest; reducing stress, helping to reduce your heart rate and blood pressure and feel more relaxed. Improving the quality and duration of your sleep, allowing you to wake up feeling refreshed and energized. Boosting your mood by releasing endorphins, the body's natural feel-good chemicals.

And then there is the spiritual aspect of our approach. The spiritual element is woven into all that we share. We don't consider spirituality to be religious in any way - we are referring to reconnecting with yourself, with the wisdom and intuition that sits within all of us. This may feel uncomfortable, even a little scary. Let those thoughts go and allow us to gently guide you through.

You will go on an exciting journey of self-discovery. We will help you to identify what has been negatively influencing you up until now, what makes you anxious, so that you can step out of that version of yourself and into more of what makes you happy, feel safe and at peace.

We want to point out that there *is* another version of you. We know people often worry that if they shed their anxiety who will they be? As if, somehow, they will lose themselves. That simply is not true.

Some parts of this journey are going to be emotional. We have witnessed that bitter-sweet moment with many clients when they finally identify all the emotional baggage they have been hauling around with them over the years and then finally letting it go. There are often tears – tears of sadness for what they have put themselves through, but very quickly tears of relief and ultimately joy at being able to shed the weight of both the limiting and negative self-beliefs.

How to use this Book

We have shared the essence of our approach so now we want to share how the PRISM Program is structured and how to use the tools and techniques to get the most from it.

What you are looking to do is create a routine dedicated to going through our PRISM method. Take a moment and think about when you have an hour each week. We encourage you to protect this time and re-arrange things that come up that may clash. You deserve to carve out this small amount of time for yourself.

Doing something just for yourself can be quite hard but equally liberating. It will be easier to make the excuse that 'so and so needs me' so I missed my reading time today. That there is self-sabotage. We will be talking about this and how to properly care for yourself later in the book but start now by making a commitment to yourself to find the time for this.

So, PRISM has 5 modules for you to follow, each of these builds on the last. Taken as a whole, it will generate powerful and lasting change.

You can work through the book as many times as you want, allowing you to work through all the scenarios that are not serving you. You have made a brave choice, and you will make shifts as a result.

You need to give yourself time and space to grow and feel comfortable with the shifts in your mindset. If you don't, you may find yourself stuck in repetitive patterns of thinking.

Each module includes a series of coaching techniques plus an exercise to complete. You will find each exercise has an accompanying workbook. Be sure to keep all your workbooks and notes in a safe place after completing each exercise as we refer to them in later sessions.

The techniques often require you to write down your own experiences and thoughts. It is important to follow the instructions rather than just thinking about the answers in your head, as the act of forming the words and writing them down allows you to create neural pathways that create new habits. Using a blue ink pen works the best, this works on the memory centre of the brain, the hippocampus. Our neural transmitters are more stimulated by colour, especially the blue end of the spectrum.

It is important to follow the chapters in order, unless otherwise advised, as PRISM has been designed to gradually build on the previous exercises; allowing you to shift your way of thinking and feeling and to take back control step by step. Trust the process. Even if you can't see why at the time. Life is always understood more fully in hindsight.

Make sure to find a quiet place to work through the book, where you will not be disturbed and can feel relaxed. To get the most from the sessions, give your full attention and do not listen to the Reiki or the visualisation exercises whilst driving. You can find all audio materials and workbooks at https://direction.academy/prism.

The Program has been created to allow you to make small incremental changes that are long lasting and sustainable rather than quick fixes. We call out anyone who wants to take your money for the promise of an instant fix as there is no such thing. Be patient and give yourself the time you need. Every week you will be making positive shifts in the way you think and feel.

It's Just Head Hoo-Ha

We delve into techniques to help you change your mindset and to identify positive input to give your brain, so you can take back control. We look at exercise, nutrition, the tools in your wellbeing toolkit. We explore modalities like mindfulness, Reiki, meditation, and how to give yourself time and space to relax, release and renew.

Here's just some of what the tools and techniques you will learn will help you to achieve:

- Discover how to change your perspective and let go of self-limiting beliefs that perpetuate anxious thoughts.
- Gain insight into the origin of your anxiety and learn how to think more positively.
- Break free from the patterns of guilt, fear, shame, frustration, and disappointment that are holding you back.
- Uncover the power of your subconscious mind and harness it to make lasting changes in your thinking and behaviour.
- Cultivate self-compassion and become your own best friend, rather than your worst enemy.
- Learn to say 'no' without guilt and start prioritizing your needs and desires.
- Develop a strong sense of self-trust, no longer seeking validation or approval from others.
- Release both the emotional and physical symptoms of anxiety, finding comfort in your body and mind.
- Experience improved sleep and wake up feeling refreshed and energized.
- Enjoy increased happiness, love, resilience, control, confidence, and serenity.

There are 5 modules in the PRISM method: Modules two and three, Release and Invite, have been combined as they need to be worked together, as you will see once you get started.

Module one: Prepare. To make and sustain long lasting changes it is important to fully prepare for the change. We start by understanding what is currently going on for you, identifying the way you want to think, feel and behave and then start to shift your mindset. We will show you how to prepare yourself.

Module two: Release. We will guide you through how to let go of the thoughts, feelings and emotions that are getting in your way, that undermine your self-confidence, make you feel low, cause stress and anxiety or hold you back from doing the things you want to do. We will share some very simple ways to release disempowering thoughts, feelings and emotions.

Module three: Invite. This is where you get to invite what you DO want. Then you can start to create how you want to feel, think, and behave.

Module four: Shift. We look at how you can shift from just inviting change to making it happen using a range of very practical techniques.

Module five: Maintain. This is the final stage in the PRISM framework. We will look at lifestyle changes you can introduce to help you maintain your emotional and physical wellbeing and keep moving forward.

What is Anxiety?

The way anxiety manifests is different for every person, and so are the scenarios that may act as triggers.

There are eight broad categories of anxiety. These are not exclusive as you may experience symptoms from more than one form of anxiety and of course, each one can vary in severity.

Generalized Anxiety Disorder (GAD): You experience excessive worry or fear about various aspects of life, such as work, relationships, or health. Your thoughts are on a loop, going round and round in your head. You find it difficult to control your worries, and this can then interfere with day-to-day life.

Social Anxiety Disorder (SAD): You experience intense fear or anxiety in social situations, such as meeting new people, public speaking, or attending social gatherings. You constantly fear being judged, embarrassed, or humiliated, which often leads to you avoiding social interactions.

Panic Disorder: You experience panic attacks; episodes of intense fear or discomfort that reach their peak within minutes. During panic attacks your heart races, you may sweat, tremble, find yourself short of breath, and feel a sense of impending doom. Panic disorder is often accompanied by agoraphobia, which is the fear of being in situations or places where escape might be difficult or embarrassing.

Obsessive-Compulsive Disorder (OCD): You experience unwanted and intrusive thoughts, called obsessions, that lead to repetitive behaviours or mental acts, known as compulsions. You feel driven to perform these compulsions to temporarily relieve your anxiety, but this behaviour can become repetitive and therefore take up a lot of time and energy, which is when it impacts your daily life.

Post-Traumatic Stress Disorder (PTSD): PTSD may develop if you have experienced or witnessed a traumatic event. You may have flashbacks, nightmares, intrusive thoughts, or intense distress when exposed to reminders of the traumatic event. You may also experience hypervigilance, avoidance of certain places or situations, and emotional numbness.

Specific Phobias: You experience an intense and fear of a specific object, situation, or activity. For example, fear of heights, spiders, flying, or needles. You tend to avoid the fear-inducing situations, which can interfere with daily life.

Separation Anxiety: This is most seen in children, but it can also occur in adults. It involves excessive fear or worry about separation from attachment figures, such as parents or caregivers. You experience significant distress when separated from loved ones and so avoid being alone.

High-functioning anxiety: You struggle with overthinking, self-criticism, overwhelm, difficulty saying no, people-pleasing, over-working, difficulty relaxing, and burnout.

No matter what shape or form your anxiety takes the key thing to understand is that anxiety is triggered by a fear of either something that has happened or a fear of something that we believe may happen. As the different forms of anxiety illustrate, we experience many types of fear; Fear of ridicule, of judgment or criticism, of being alone, abandoned, not loved, not liked or of not being good enough. And it will be one or many of these fears that underlies your anxiety.

It's Just Head Hoo-Ha

These fears are buried deep within your subconscious and rarely form as conscious thought. However, they lurk in the recesses of your brain shaping the way you respond.

In every situation we find ourselves in, our brain runs through a pattern to check whether it is safe and whether it is the same or like something we have experienced before. At times it will make connections between old and new events that wouldn't seem logical to our conscious brain. Connections back to events where one of our fears was triggered and we felt unsafe or vulnerable.

Once this happens our brain interprets the new scenario as 'dangerous'. If we then have an increased emotional response to the perceived 'danger', our brain stores this as something to watch out for and warn us of in the future. That is when the tell-tale signs of anxiety can start to present themselves.

The fears we refer to here are deep-seated and not recognisable in the way your anxiety manifests. Instead, you may experience one or many of these physical, cognitive, or emotional symptoms:

Your heart races.
Your blood pressure increases,
You breathe more quickly and shallowly.
You feel sweaty, shaky, or short of breath.
You feel lightheaded.
You feel overwhelmed and unable to cope.
You feel lonely or isolated.
You feel guilty.
Feel tired all the time, poor sleep.
You lose your appetite, reduced sex drive.
You experience muscular aches and pains or reoccurring illness.
You ruminate or catastrophise.

Whatever your experience is, it feels very real and can be very distressing. So, as well as looking into the root cause for your anxiety we will explore how calming your body will allow you to calm your mind. Our emotional response triggers a physical response and vice versa, therefore we need to address both to restore harmony.

It's Just Head Hoo-Ha

The Science Bit

Before we get started on the different modules within the PRISM method, we thought it would be useful to talk about what is going on inside our brain and body and how these finely balanced systems can and do affect your wellbeing.

We are not going to go into too much scientific detail, but it is good to know about some of the different factors that affect your brain activity to help you understand how and why the techniques within PRISM work.

Our brain is made up of a complicated network of over ten billion cells, called neurons. These neurons are constantly transmitting and receiving messages both from activity within our body and from external stimuli, via our senses of sight, sound, smell, taste and touch. Every thought and feeling you experience, everything you do, is a result of this brain activity.

This is how you make sense of the world. Your whole body works with your brain to help you stay safe. However, sometimes your brain senses danger where there isn't any, making us feel anxious or panicky when there is no cause to.

For our brain to work well everything must be in balance. That means the right number of neurotransmitters (the messengers sending and receiving messages between neurons) must be released in the right part of our brain to allow it to correctly interpret the messages it receives and to send the right messages in response.

In other words, if there are too few neurotransmitters our brain may not send a message and if there are too many, the wrong message may be received. Where in the brain any imbalance in neurotransmitters occurs will impact how we respond to events.

From the moment we are born our brains are learning. They do this by looking for repeating patterns in our experiences and trying different responses to those experiences. For example, when a baby hears their parents talking to them, they will attempt to respond with a noise in reply. Often a coo or a gurgle initially. As the baby continues to hear their parents' voices, learning different sounds and words, over time those cooing and gurgling noises become more sophisticated, and the baby begins to talk.

Throughout, babies are normally rewarded with words of encouragement, smiles and cuddles, giving them the motivation to keep developing. As adults we are also responding to internal and external stimuli and our brains are continually learning, changing and adapting. This is very important to note because, whilst logically we are aware that stress and anxiety inducing situations can be handled calmly and effectively by some people, others have learnt to respond with panic and fear.

They have formed neural pathways that are not serving them well. However, we can unlearn current behaviours to make way for new behaviours and ways of thinking - particularly when we put some emotion behind it.

As Donald Hebb said: 'Neurons that fire together, wire together'. In other words, whenever we have an initially strong reaction to something and then repeat the response, we strengthen that pathway in our brain. If we continue to feel anxious, stressed or unhappy we strengthen that pathway and make it easier to replicate these feelings to the point where this becomes our default way of thinking.

It's Just Head Hoo-Ha

The good news is that we can take back control and over-ride the automatic responses our brains have learnt. To create new patterns of thinking through what is known as neuro or brain plasticity. Plasticity refers to our brain's ability to adapt and change and to make new connections. Part of this is unlearning stress responses that are not working for us. In effect, we can become our own teachers and teach ourselves to respond without anxiety or negativity.

There are two types of neuroplasticity: **Functional** – this is when the brain moves a function from a damaged area to an undamaged area of the brain.

Structural – this is when the brain makes changes to its physical structure through learning and memory. You are going to use your brain's natural structural plasticity.

Two key things here are repetition and the intensity of feeling. The strength of feeling is important – the more intensely you feel something, the stronger the brain activity. Add some repetition to strengthen this and bingo, things really start to change.

Dr Kim and Dr Hil have reported that by the time we hit 35 up to 90% of what we think, feel and do is recycled from our past. Our brain is lazy and likes to repeat things as this requires less effort. The familiar, default way of thinking or behaving is a well-worn neural pathway and so the easiest to travel back down. But by learning to respond without anxiety or negativity, you can swap out your current default pathway.

The cognitive techniques, which are broadly based on CBT (Cognitive Behavioural therapy) and NLP (Neurolinguistic Programming), coupled with the Reiki and meditative practices we share, exploit the brain's structural plasticity to develop new connections between neurons.

Let's take a deeper look at the role of neurotransmitters. Let's first look at what happens when we have too few neurotransmitters. Research has shown that people who experience anxiety and depression often have depleted levels of Serotonin. Serotonin has been labelled as one of the 'feel good' hormones as it plays a vital role in regulating our mood. Stopping us from worrying and feeling low. Maintaining a healthy appetite, controlling impulses and regulating our sleep and perception of pain.

The neurotransmitter gamma aminobutyric acid (GABA) helps to calm activity in our nervous system and so if we do not have sufficient GABA we can find ourselves mentally and physically over-reacting to situations that we would otherwise have not responded to.

Likewise, not enough dopamine, the hormone involved in the 'pleasure and reward' pathway of the brain, can cause us to feel low, lonely and demotivated. We can also find it difficult to stay focused. Our world is hard-wired to produce stress/reward responses which can become a rollercoaster of neural addiction. Learning to calm some of these responses gives you better control over your response to everything.

We will be looking at how diet and exercise can naturally boost your levels of Serotonin and Dopamine, as well as introducing techniques that can help trigger the pleasure/reward response. It's a fact that if you put diesel in a petrol car it breaks down. The same goes for your diet and you.

Having too many neurotransmitters can also cause us problems. When we respond to a perceived stressful situation, we release noradrenaline and Cortisol, but if we release too much this can lead to tension and panic.

Similarly, if we have too much Dopamine in the thinking part of our brain – known as the prefrontal cortex – we can find ourselves stuck in a cycle of negative thinking. We remember bad feelings we have linked to memories, which is what can cause us to panic or experience social anxiety when we are faced with a similar situation or pull us down into feelings of despair.

We explore how we can over-ride these automatic responses by deliberately engaging our pre-frontal cortex to give our brains a different message. Over time, with repetition this creates new neural pathways, this then becomes the way our brain knows to respond.

We experience many different situations our brain interprets as a threat, some of which are caused by a real and present danger but many more are triggered by our thoughts and feelings. Our brains have not yet evolved to differentiate between the two types of threat. This means the part of our brain called the amygdala, will initiate the 'fight, flight, or freeze' response in both scenarios. It increases blood flow and directs more white blood cells to the neural pathway associated with that train of thought. If the same response is repeated our brains will store the thought as something important to be remembered and repeated. The next time the same thing or something our brain interprets as similar happens, our brains will try to initiate the same panicky or anxious response. And the more this happens, the more it happens.

Interestingly there is a study that compares the expected threat response in indigenous people who live with the threat of animal attack in the jungle with our neural response to daily stimulation in the modern world. Even just our phones notifications that ping constantly take us into threat mode. They found that the indigenous person had much more freedom from threat than a person living in a city with all its stimulation, even though the threat to life in a city doesn't include being eaten by a tiger or a huge snake and isn't a life of just mere survival.

What we will be doing is showing you that the negative thought patterns your brain experiences are not significant anymore. In the same way your brain used repetition to create this negative response, you can use repetition to respond in a calm, relaxed and controlled way.

Sex hormones also have a part to play here. Too little testosterone has been linked with increased anxiety. Not only that, but testosterone also plays a role in moderating the release of Cortisol. So, when testosterone levels are low, we may find our levels of the stress hormone Cortisol increase. The female sex hormone, oestrogen may also be linked to anxiety symptoms. This is why women may find their anxiety levels are impacted at certain times during their menstrual cycle and during menopause. If you believe this may be happening, it is a good idea to keep a record of what is happening during a typical menstrual cycle. You can then decide whether you want to discuss this with your medical Doctor.

We will look at how we can naturally boost testosterone and a chemical called Oxytocin to help combat the effect of some of our hormonal deficiencies. Finally, if you have an over-active thyroid, you may find you experience more of the physical symptoms linked to stress and anxiety.

Everything is just Energy

Imagine yourself cocooned inside a big ball of energy – like one of those washing up liquid bubbles, transparent but with beautiful rainbow colours at the edges. Pause for a moment and if you can, imagine positive energy quickly buzzing through and around you, allowing you to feel vibrant, alert, confident, resilient, at ease with who you are and capable of anything. This is the energy you want to hold on to. The energy you want to invite more of, to expand and to propel you towards living your best life.

Conversely, your bubble also has disempowering energy slowing you down, that manifests as negative chatter in your head, that undermines your self-confidence, that can make you feel tired, unhappy, worried, anxious, stressed, doubtful or overly self-critical. This is the negative energy we are going to help you release.

We will use several different techniques throughout the 5 modules of PRISM, but at the core of our approach is the principle that our thoughts, feelings and emotions are just energy …

Physics shows us that everything, including humans, are basically just energy. When you understand this on a deeper level you can influence your energy by how you think and act.

All of us radiate energy. We all carry around both positive and negative energy. It is created and stored based on your individual life events. Every word, act, or deed you have experienced, since the day you were born will have been linked to an emotion – good or bad - and stored in your subconscious mind as a reference for you to interpret and respond to the world.

This means you will have, like every other human being, a lot of unsupportive self-beliefs stored. These are thoughts, feelings and emotions that can hold you back from living your best life, cause you to sabotage making big life changes and create anxiety, low mood, doubt, or fear.

We also mirror the energy of the people around us so the negative energy of others in your life may be having an impact on you and vice versa.

We recognise that the idea of *your* energy impacting those around you, may concern you. We will explain more later in the book but for now, know that having anxiety does not mean you make those around you feel anxious. We are referring to behaviours that are overtly or repeatedly negative, critical, or judgemental, as these carry more energetic weight.

To fully step into your personal power and feel in flow you need to let go of these limiting self-beliefs, release your negative chatter and your disempowering thoughts and feelings and increase your emotional vibration. Once you start recognising yourself as an energetic being, you will shift the negative thoughts and feelings much more easily.

Your Emotional Vibration

Have you ever walked into a room and just instinctively felt tension? The energy in the room feels heavy, prickly. We talk about being able to 'cut the atmosphere with a knife'. That's because every emotion we experience has a vibration. The more disempowering the emotion the lower its' vibrational frequency. Fear and hate are the lowest vibrating and so feel heavy and dark, lacking in energy.

At the other end of the vibrational scale is love. Love allows us to feel happy and confident, full of energy, light and free. To feel in a state of harmony and flow you need to be at the higher end of the emotional scale.

We like to think of being 'in harmony' as being in a state of optimum health, happiness, and vitality, whereby you have released disempowering thoughts and invited in higher vibrating thoughts, feelings and emotions; Where you have a ball of positive energy around you (remember that bubble), so that when you bump up against life's challenges – which realistically you will continue to do – you can let them bounce off you more easily.

Our PRISM method guides you through releasing the thoughts, feelings and emotions that hold you back and keep you in a negative cycle, helping you to invite more positive energy and allow you to make life-changing transformations. PRISM teaches you to release your negative chatter and become more confident, more resilient, and more self-accepting.

Most importantly, before you start your transformational journey, leave all judgement behind. Judgement of yourself and judgement of others. There is no right or wrong here; Accept things are just as they are. Don't waste any energy on judgement.

Judging and being judged is an inherent part of our human experience. What we don't see is just how much energy we waste on it. We use judgement as a form of self-sabotage. By focusing on what we dislike about others we don't have to put the energy into ourselves or into something positive.

We will help you to better understand and work this through as you absorb the guidance we offer in this book.

It's Just Head Hoo-Ha

Junilda Wright

Module One:
P for Prepare

Junilda Wright

PREPARE

You are planning a two-week holiday abroad. There are certain things you need to do in advance to ensure your travel plans go well. You will need a valid passport, any necessary visas, pack suitable clothing, book a flight, a place to stay etc. In short, you prepare. Without this kind of preparation, you are not going to get very far.

It is no different when it comes to your emotional and physical wellbeing. To C.R.E.A.T.E and sustain long lasting changes you need to fully prepare for the change. So, throughout this module we will be showing you how to prepare yourself.

There are six steps in the prepare module, each one building on the last to allow you to C.R.E.A.T.E transformational change. We will explain what each letter of the acronym stands for in a moment.

The exercises we are going to guide you through in this module will allow you to understand where you currently are, where you want to be and start the process of welcoming in more happiness, confidence, resilience, contentment, positive expectation, self-acceptance, calm and peace of mind.

We set the pace and guide you throughout the process, step by step. All lasting change happens in baby steps, so bring your focus to just the task in hand. Recognise if you are trying to rush or are fixating on the result rather than the process. All you need to do is keep reading and complete the exercises.

So, what does **C.R.E.A.T.E** stand for?

C is for Current story. We each have a story that tells of who we are and what we believe. Our individual story is a powerful way to understand what is currently going on for each of us.

You can see this as the way to acknowledge your current struggles. To understand your current thoughts, feelings, and emotions and to expose the limiting beliefs we all hold because of our conditioning, our environment, our biological make-up, past traumas and our life experiences. These beliefs, which are stored in your subconscious brain, influence your feelings of self-worth and self-identity; shaping the way you currently think and respond to the world. It is critical that you bring awareness to this to be able to make transformational change. If you don't identify the cause you can't deal with it.

So, we will start by describing your current story – what is currently going on for you? What do you want to change and why? We will guide you through how to do this in the next chapter.

If, for example you experience social anxiety - in this module you would explore which social situations make you feel anxious. What thoughts, feelings and emotions come up for you before, during and/or after social occasions, how this impacts you and how you believe others are affected. When your anxiety began and why it is important to you to change how you feel and behave.

We often do not give ourselves the space we need to reflect properly on how we feel or to fully process our thoughts, feelings and emotions. Even with friends and family, there is huge pressure to 'get over it' and get 'back to normal'.

When we suppress or ignore something that has affected us, all we do is store it up for a bigger crash in the future. Therefore, until you acknowledge where you are now and the thoughts and

It's Just Head Hoo-Ha

feelings you are holding onto, it is almost impossible to know where you want or need to go next.

It is important to note to not become entangled in your thoughts. Do not get caught up in negative internal dialogue but do give yourself time to process your thoughts, feelings, and emotions.

Giving yourself a little time to process a situation is time well spent in the long run as you have dealt with the situation there and then. You start to bring this level of awareness by writing out your current story and begin to fully understand how you are feeling and what you are thinking. You can then start to make positive shifts to release and let go of the things that are not serving you.

R is for replacement story. How you would like things to be. How you want to feel. This is your replacement story.

During this step, you will address each point you described in your current story and turn it into a positive. Your replacement story is about understanding what it is *you* want; How *you* want to think, feel and behave. To reveal what *you* need, which you may not even be aware of right now. All as preparation for a shift in your mindset.

E is for emotional engagement. We explore tools to help you to emotionally engage with your goal. The more emotionally engaged you are, the more likely you are to want to keep going and make the changes needed. This is very different from emotional entanglement which is a downward spiral that holds you in a repetitive pattern – not being able to move on from the past and into the life you want.

A is for Achievement Target. The first emotional engagement tool will be to create an achievement target. This will help to keep you motivated, as there may be times when you will want to give up, even though you know this would mean reverting to your old way of thinking and feeling. We will talk about the pendulum swing between wanting change and reverting back to old behaviours as we move through the chapters.

T is for trigger statements. You will also create what we call trigger statements. These help you to start to trigger your new patterns of thinking. Through daily repetition you will develop new neural pathways and train your brain to create new ways of responding to life.

E is for Envisage. We reinforce all of this by envisaging the future… creating a mental picture of how you want to feel and respond. We create our life through our hopes and dreams. This is the first and most important step. So, we will be helping you to start to imagine a different way of being so that this can become your reality.

Let's get started!

C is for Current Story

We are going to start with you describing your current story, which we will guide you through, but, before you go any further, you need - as we said previously, and we can't emphasize this enough – to leave negative judgement at the door. You need to allow thoughts, feelings, and emotions to come and go without judging them, yourself or others.

Say the phrase '*It is what it is*' to yourself to avoid any kind of judgement. It will take some practice, but as you work through the five modules of PRISM and exercise your 'allowance muscle' it will become easier and easier.

The purpose of this section is to allow you to own your life story. Only then will you have the power to live as you really want to.

As we described in the previous chapter, before you initiate any change, no matter what it is, no matter how big or small - you need to understand where you currently are and to bring awareness to what is going on for you, and where you have come from. It is an important part of your journey to acknowledge your early influences and how they created a subconscious blueprint that runs like a hidden app in your brain, draining your battery and holding you in a cycle.

As we mentioned previously, we want to make the distinction between processing thoughts, feelings and emotions versus becoming entangled in them. What we will be doing here, is giving you the space to *process* them. We refer to this as understanding 'your current story'.

What is it about your current way of thinking and behaving that you want to change and what will making that change mean for you? What was it that was holding you back or stopping you from taking or maintaining action? During this exercise you will start to expose your negative chatter and those disempowering and limiting beliefs. By exposing them, you can see what needs shifting and thereby reduce their power over you.

Okay let's start to C.R.E.A.T.E your story.

We strongly recommend choosing just one aspect of your life or one scenario to focus on to begin with. Choose a less impactful scenario to start.

We understand you're most likely impatient to see the changes, but if you try to change too many things at once, the chances of success are more limited, and you are likely to become overwhelmed.

The first rule of PRISM Club is to allow time for the integration of the shifts you will be making. We rarely give ourselves time to process the things that happen to us, which is how they become subconscious beliefs and run our lives in a chaotic way.

So, for example if you experience social anxiety, choose just one scenario that is a trigger for you, such as meeting up with friends in a restaurant, rather than tackling your social anxiety as a whole.

Once you feel comfortable with how this process works, you can repeat it multiple times to address every stress inducing or self-deprecating scenario. And the more you do it, the quicker you will experience results and the more natural it will become.

So, we want you to either download the workbooks which you can find at https://direction.academy/prism or write down the different headings you will find in the workbooks on the top of separate pages in your own notepad. This is your story, so whichever you choose, be sure to keep your content in a safe place where nobody else can read it. Do not share what you have written with anybody else.

Start this exercise when you have at least 40 minutes to yourself. Choose a space where you will not be interrupted, where you feel relaxed and can be yourself. This can be emotional, so give yourself the time and space you need.

Now take a few deep breaths in and out, bringing your breath right down into your abdomen each time and extending the out breath.

Shrug your shoulders up to your ears and then down.

Gently, squeeze your shoulder blades closer together to widen across your collar bones.

Take another breath, even deeper this time and as you exhale imagine the air coursing all the way down to the soles of your feet.

Feel the ground holding you. Take a few breaths here and feel more grounded and relaxed with each one.

Smile!

Okay, you are ready to start.

What change do you want to make?

We invite you to write down what it is that you want to change in as much detail as you can. Remember no judgement!

Ask yourself '*why is this important to me?*' Once you have answered that ask yourself '*why that is important?*' and once again '*why that is important?*'

For example:
I want to feel less overwhelmed and panicky at work.
Why?
Because it is impacting my health.
Why is your health important?
Because I don't feel myself and find I am getting short tempered with my partner and kids.
Why is that important?
It's impacting my relationship with them. I can see they don't like it when I shout, and I always end up hating myself for shouting.
Why does that matter?
I don't want them to not like me, I love them, and I want to like myself.

Keep going until you feel you have dug down into the heart of what you want to change. Don't worry if you have not peeled back many layers on your first attempt, you can always revisit this again. There is no right or wrong way of doing this.

How is this impacting you and others?

Describe how this scenario is impacting your life. For now, try to forget thinking you should or should not feel a certain way. Just be honest. Describe the impact you believe this is having on you and the people around you.

So, for example:

I often feel overwhelmed in social situations. I want to meet up with friends but the thought of having to go into a bar or restaurant to meet them fills me with dread. I end up pulling out at the last minute to avoid those feelings which means I am seeing less and less of my friends.

I am worried they will stop inviting me out or stop talking to me and I will lose their friendship.

Sometimes I feel they don't like me or that I am boring. I feel distant from my group of friends. I feel left out of a lot of their jokes these days as I rarely see them. This makes me unhappy and isolated. I feel low.

Thoughts, feelings, and emotions

Now think about how your current situation makes you feel. It's easy to be judgemental here. Try not to go there, instead just focus on the thoughts, emotions and feelings. Be completely honest with yourself. We often shy away from what we call 'dirty' emotions — emotions we feel we should not be feeling like resentment, jealousy or dislike. Ask yourself what you 'think' is going to happen? What are your fears around this?

Remember this is only between you and your workbook. Nobody else will know. It is very important to capture your true feelings, no matter what they are, so that you can release them. If your story includes other people, describe how they affect you and what you perceive to be happening. Try to use full sentences to put each one into context rather than just a list.

Let's take a work example:

I feel under pressure a lot of the time at work. There always seems to be more to do than I have hours in the day for. This makes me feel overwhelmed.

I feel tired most of the time. I feel drained when I think about all the things I need to do. I wake up feeling this way.

Always feeling tired is really getting me down. I don't feel I can join in with the office banter as I am pre-occupied with all the things I need to do.

Sometimes I feel physically sick. I worry that my colleagues think I am unsociable or boring. I worry that my line manager is not happy with the quality of my work and that I am taking too long to complete my responsibilities. I find it hard to concentrate. I get frustrated and fed up. I often feel I don't want to go into work.

Versus a list…I feel under-pressure, I feel tired, I feel drained, I feel down, I feel sick, I feel worried, I feel frustrated, I feel fed up.

Just writing a list doesn't give you any deeper clarity about *why* you feel this way or *where* you want to be.

By writing the full description, you will be able see the different parts to your story – in the example, there are feelings associated with having too much to do and feelings linked to colleagues and the line manager. Again, this is about digging out the root cause. We will come back to how to review your story later once you have completed it.

If you are finding it difficult to write what you believe to be your full story - just write what you can for now. You can always revisit this.

In fact, we recommend taking it slowly. When we have a lot to shift, we can only handle bite sized pieces. Each time we release negativity, even though it is a good thing, we still need time to emotionally repair.

That is why you need to do this at a steady pace - making small, incremental changes, otherwise you will find it too much and most likely just give up.

What has held you back?

Next, we would like you to think about what has held you back from making changes to your situation.

It may be that you feel you don't know how to change things, or you feel powerless to make changes and that's okay. It may be linked to money or time. Whatever your reasons, we can almost guarantee these are very human responses. Remember this is not to judge, just to understand. Think about your day-to-day routine and all the other factors of your life such as partners, friends, commitments and finances.

Following on from the work example you might write "*I don't have time to make changes. I don't even know what I could change. I need to work as we need the money.*"

It's Just Head Hoo-Ha

What other thoughts pop into your head when you think about your story?

Try and write down as much detail as possible. When did this start? How did you feel back then? Is it different to how you feel now? If so, in what way is it different?

Physical feelings

Now think about and write down any physical sensations you experience when you feel anxious or panicky.

Do you break into a sweat? Does your heart start to race, your breathing become faster and shallower? Do you feel faint? Does your face or body flush? Do you feel nauseous? Do you feel tingly? Do you feel a pain in your chest or experience a sinking feeling in the pit of your stomach? Do you feel weighed down and heavy? Do you feel tired and drained? Do you have illnesses that crop up at certain times or with certain triggers? E.g., always being ill at Christmas or when you have time off work.

What other, seemingly unrelated thoughts pop into your head when you experience your anxiety, panic or negative spiral? Can you link it back to something else that is happening or has happened in your life?

When you feel you have your current story on paper - take a few moments to take a few deep breaths.

Relax your shoulders down away from your ears. If you need to, tell yourself you are okay a few times.

Well done. This can be an emotional process. A vital thing to understand right here is that 'it is what it is'. Your life has evolved to bring you here.

This isn't the time to take a journey into hating your life or yourself, rather to be the observer of your life as if you were an actor in a film.

In the next chapter we will guide you through creating your replacement story – you will be re-writing the script. In other words, how would you like things to be? How would you like to feel?

We have recorded a guided Reiki session to help you relax and start to feel calmer. Visit https://direction.academy/prism to listen. We recommend listening just before bed to aid restful sleep.

R is for Replacement Story

In the previous chapter you described your current story and the associated thoughts, feelings, and emotions. You started to reveal your current way of thinking and to understand which patterns in your current mindset need to change. It is important that this awareness has been brought to your current thought patterns to allow you to change them.

If you are continuing to read this straight after the previous chapter – great! If not, we suggest you re-read your current story all the way through. Remember the feelings and emotions that caused you to write those statements.

We would now like you to turn your attention to how you want your life to be and how you want to think and feel. Your replacement story will help you to start to create new positive ways of thinking.

We often focus on what we don't want. However, in this exercise, we will guide you through how to be clear about what you DO want.

For example, *"I want to feel relaxed and happy travelling to and from work and learn to enjoy this time in my day"* as opposed to: *"I don't want to feel anxious travelling to and from work"*.

This may seem like simple semantics, but the language we use is very important to the way our subconscious responds to the message.

In the second example our subconscious hears 'anxious', whereas in the first it hears 'relaxed and happy'. **Very different messages.**

A more Spiritual aspect of this work is learning how we create our lives first with our thoughts and then we literally speak our life into creation.

For example, saying things like: "Nothing ever works out for me", sadly it would appear as though it doesn't. Saying something over and over to yourself and to anyone who will listen, leads you to believe it is a reality.

So, we would like you to turn to the **Replacement Story** section of your Prepare workbook. Focus just on the topic you described in the current story exercise.

As before - only start this exercise when you have at least 40 minutes to yourself. Choose a space where you will not be interrupted, where you feel you can relax and be yourself.

As you go through this exercise of creating your 'replacement story' try to avoid limiting thoughts like 'I can't do that because…', 'that didn't work before so…'.

If you can, start to believe that any and everything is possible. You can work on the practicalities later. For now, allow yourself to imagine your dream scenario.

Don't think that you must know how it's going to happen for you at this point - that will put that big brain of yours into another cycle. This is your chance to dream and believe in the magic of the world.

One other thing we want to steer you away from is any kind of vengeful desire. If your current story involves people who you feel have hurt you, just allow them to be who they are. We will cover how to release these types of thoughts, feelings and emotions later.

Okay, let's get started. Take a few slow, deep breaths in and out. Draw out the exhale. Relax. Smile. Allow your imagination free reign.

What I want to achieve

When you are ready, write down what it is you want to achieve. Choose your language carefully. It is important that you describe the way you want things to be in the positive, rather than what you don't want to happen or described in double negatives.

Go ahead and start to write the first three or four sentences on what you want to achieve, referring to what you wrote in your Current story.

Remember the language you use is very important as your subconscious brain – where all the limiting beliefs and negative chatter comes from – does not 'hear' the negatives. Avoid words like 'not', 'don't', 'can't'.

Almost every client we have coached uses these negatives in their first attempt, so we would like you to reread what you write and check again for negatives. We are doubling up on this point as it is both important and enlightening to catch ourselves, subconsciously, letting the negatives in.

Here's an example of what **not** to write:

I don't want to be stressed. I don't want to shout at my kids. I don't want to feel overwhelmed and under pressure. I want to stop feeling weak and insecure.

In this example, your subconscious would hear, 'stressed… shout at my kids' etc, which of course, is exactly what you don't want.

Putting this to one side, using double negatives or avoidant language is much less empowering. There always seems to be an underlying hint of judgement with this kind of language.

Versus, an example of a more supportive statement:

'I want to be calm, relaxed and in control of my day. I want to feel good. I want to have a great relationship with my partner and kids. I want to like myself'.

Just take a moment to re-read what you have written so far to make sure it is all stated in the positive.

Now continue to describe what it is you **do** want.

Your motivation

Next, write down what will happen when you make the change. What impact will this have on your life? This is where your motivation to make the necessary changes is going to come from.

Go back and look at what you wrote under the 'How is this impacting you and others?' section in the previous exercise to make sure you have addressed each point you put down as positive statements here. Remember to describe how you <u>want</u> to think, feel, and behave.

Some examples of how to switch to positive statements:

Current story	**Replacement story**
I often feel overwhelmed and distant from my family	**I feel in control and connected to my family**
The thought of having to go into a bar or restaurant to meet friends fills me with dread	**I feel relaxed and happy about meeting my friends in a bar or restaurant**
I am sure they avoid me.	**I feel they like spending**

It's Just Head Hoo-Ha

Sometimes I feel they don't like me	**time with me**
We never seem to talk anymore or do anything fun together	**We have fun together**
This makes me unhappy and isolated	**I feel happy and connected**
I often feel I don't want to go into work.	**I look forward to going to work**
I feel low	**I feel good**

Who, apart from you, will this positively impact? How will it impact them?

One thing to point out here is that you cannot change how other people feel. You are not responsible for other people's thoughts, feelings, or emotions, so avoid stating how you want anybody other than yourself to feel. We will look at your relationship with others in more detail later.

This will impact my friendships. I will be able to meet up with them more regularly and be a more active member of our social circle. I will feel more connected and relaxed when I am socialising with my friends.

Thoughts, Feelings and Emotions

Continue describing how you want to feel about yourself and your situation. Again, make sure you address each point you outlined in the previous exercise.

Disempowering	**Empowering**
I feel under pressure a lot of the time at work	**I have enough time to do all the things I need to get done.**
Sometimes this makes me feel	**I am in control**

overwhelmed	
I feel tired most of the time	**I feel energised**
I feel drained when I think about all the things I need to do. I wake up feeling this way	**I wake up feeling refreshed and ready for the day**
Always feeling tired is really getting me down and I feel I am not there for my partner or kids	**I feel on top of things. I feel happy. I am there for my partner and kids**
I get frustrated and fed up	**I feel relaxed and happy**
I feel distant from my family / friends / colleagues.	**I feel connected to my family / friends /colleagues**
I feel I cannot tell them how I feel. I don't even really know why I feel this way.	**I am comfortable expressing how I feel.**

Write down any other aspects to your replacement story that pop up for you. When you feel you have your replacement story written down, take some deep breaths in and out. Relax your shoulders away from ears again. Slow your breathing down and smile!

Well done! That's one of the trickiest bits completed. It can be very emotional and lead you to uncover thoughts, feelings, and emotions you may not have allowed yourself to acknowledge before.

You may be feeling that you were not able to capture your full story – that is okay. Start with what you have for now. You can repeat the PRISM modules again and again, each time may reveal more emotional layers.

You may be thinking this seems too simplistic. Yes, it is a very simple technique, but it is effective. We often assume that everything worthwhile doing is hard…it really isn't.

It is important not to rush through this exercise. Remember you are going to create new thought patterns through repetition,

It's Just Head Hoo-Ha

so you need to tell your subconscious brain how you want to think and feel. This needs to be a strong, positive message as you are taking back control.

We also want you to start to take notice of the language you are using, not just for the sake of this exercise, but in general as this again impacts the messages your brain receives. When you make these statements in the present tense, your brain responds accordingly…'Oh we are feeling relaxed and in control'. Cool!

Be aware of how you speak to/of others too. We often have a pattern of being self-depreciating and moaning about our life; this is a cultural pattern.

If you met a friend in the street and they asked how you are, how would you typically reply? Would you tell them a tale of woe? Be mindful of what you say as your words reinforce your reality to your subconscious brain repeatedly. So, change up your language to be more positive.

We recommend leaving things here for today. Be kind to yourself. You may find you feel tired at the end of your day or that additional thoughts, feelings or emotions pop up that relate to your story. If that happens you can go back and add these on.

E is for Emotional Engagement

You now have a version of your replacement story that describes how you would like to think, feel, and behave in the area you have chosen to focus on.

There's a famous saying from Heraclitus that the 'only constant is change'; which when you think about it, is true. The good news is this is also true for our brains.

Our brain is always 'looking' for repetitive patterns to develop new neural pathways. So, in the same way that your brain has learnt certain patterns of thinking that may not be serving you; through repetition you can begin to develop new, more positive patterns.

Instead of letting your brain sit in an ever repeating, negative thought cycle, you can, in effect unlearn your current story. This is where you use that big, beautiful brain to imagine and start living your best life.

Now, although our brain is open to change, change can create ambiguity and feelings of uncertainty that can undermine our self-confidence and cause us to feel nervous and resistant. Our subconscious always wants to maintain the status quo and what it already knows, even when an alternative may serve us better. So, this means you need to be well prepared to outwit your subconscious brain's attempts to sabotage your desire to make shifts in your thinking.

A very powerful way to do this, is to emotionally engage with what you want to achieve. The stronger the emotional engagement, the greater the motivation and determination is to succeed.

We will be showing you three very simple steps to create that engagement.

First, we help you to gain insight on what it is you want to achieve and why – this provides your motivation.

Second, you will create what we call triggers – these are simple positive affirmations that you will repeat every day. They act as the trigger to creating new neural pathways. You will continue to repeat them until your brain has got the message and you feel you no longer need them.

Lastly, we bring this to life in your imagination with a visualisation.

A is for Achievement

We want you create an achievement target. This will help you to keep motivated and moving forward towards your goal.

Refer to the first section of your 'replacement story'. Then ask yourself - 'why do I want to make these changes?' 'What positives will come from this change?' 'Who am I doing this for?'

On a cautionary note, if you've answered any of the above questions with 'So that someone will love me/ fancy me/ respect me/ do what I tell them; reconsider your motivations for change. This change must be for you alone and not focused on someone else's opinion or an attempt to get validation or approval from them.

If you use someone else's reaction as your motivation, you will not get your desired outcome. This must be for *your own* growth and empowerment.

Be assured though, the changes will have a positive ripple effect on those around you.

Take a few moments to craft two or three simple sentences that fully describe what you want to achieve and why, so that any time you read it, you can instantly resonate with it and feel motivated.

Make sure you include some context too, so that your brain understands the connection, rather than using generalised sentences. And remember to choose the language you use to describe what you want carefully. Use absolute positive statements – do not use avoidant phrases or double negatives.

'I want to feel calm, relaxed and in control of my day. I want to feel energized and happy. I want to have the time to do what I need to get done and to have fun with my partner and kids. I want to like myself'.

Versus

'I don't want to be stressed. I don't want to feel tired and unhappy. I don't want to feel under time pressure or not have time to have fun. I don't want to not like myself'.

As we mentioned previously the language you use will have an emotional impact as well as affect the messages being sent to your subconscious brain.

Re-read our two examples and notice how differently you feel when hearing each one. The first description sounds uplifting, powerful, and energized. The second feels disempowering - as all you are doing is focussing attention on what you *don't* want.

If you need to, take a few moments to adjust what you have written so when you read it, you feel good, and it sounds like your words. You are going to use these sentences to remind yourself of what you want to achieve, so it's important they lift you up. Imagine yourself shouting them from a mountain top!

T is for Triggers

We would like you to re-read what you wrote down as your motivation for making the changes. Re-write these in the present tense – and again, be sure to use positive, uplifting language and provide the context of your scenario. For example:

'I am happy and relaxed in all social situations. I feel comfortable meeting my friends anywhere'.

'I enjoy going to work. I have lots of energy and join in the office banter. I am in control of my workload and know I do a good job. I manage my time and energy efficiently'.

You have now created your positive triggers.

E is for Envision

Let's create some emotional engagement to reinforce what you have written by envisioning how you will feel when you achieve your goal. This will help strengthen your motivation, as you are more likely do things that make you feel good and that you have an emotional attachment to.

Imagine somebody who wants to exercise more and joins a gym. They don't enjoy it at all. After a couple of weeks, they find all the excuses to stop going. A few days later their neighbour asks if they could walk their dog for them.

This person loves dogs and jumps at the chance. They enjoy this time so much they decide to get up thirty minutes earlier each morning to take the dog out. Suddenly, they are getting the exercise they wanted, and it no longer feels like a chore!

Linking mindset to positive feelings is the easiest and quickest way to shift your life and habits.

It can take up to 90 repetitions for the neural pathway to be set in your brain, that number drops to 20 repetitions when you make the habit fun or spark a heightened emotional response.

To help you build some energy around your goal, we would like to guide you through a visualisation exercise. You can either read through this next section or visit our website at https://direction.academy/prism where we have recorded this for you. If you can, we recommend choosing to listen to the recording.

If you are not going to listen to the visualisation, read through the whole of this section first and then give it a go.

Sit back in your chair. Shrug your shoulders out. Bring them up to your ears and then down. Gently move your head down to the side, bringing your right ear closer to your shoulder, keep your shoulder down – just gently, you shouldn't feel any pain or discomfort. Then bring your head back to the centre.

Repeat on your left side. Back to the middle.

Tilt your head forward gently. To the middle. And then back ever so slightly. And back to centre.

Shrug your shoulders out again.

Close your eyes and think of the words you have just written.

Take some nice, slow, deep breaths in and out. In and out. Once more in and out.

You are feeling good. Say to yourself you feel happy. Smile to yourself.

You feel relaxed. You feel in control. You feel good about yourself.

Keep breathing nice and deeply – in and out.

You feel at peace. You feel confident. Smile again. You feel excited about the changes you are going to make.

If you can, picture yourself in your scenario feeling calm, relaxed, and happy. Bring it to life by imagining what you can see, hear, physically feel, smell and hear.

Don't worry if you can't fully picture the scene this time. We dive deeper into this technique in the next module.

If that didn't feel comfortable for you, that's okay. Remember that this is a journey and every step you take is creating shifts, no matter how small.

It's Just Head Hoo-Ha

Read your achievement target and triggers again, noticing how you feel.

We recommend repeating this visualisation step regularly as you work your way through the book. An easy way to squeeze it into your day is to practice just before drifting off to sleep.

We would like you to now write out your achievement target on three separate pieces of paper. Put these in three different places that you can access throughout your day.

You may decide to put one in your wallet, one on your bedside table and one in your car, for example. It's up to you where you put them, if they are in places you can get to. Any time you feel yourself questioning why you are making the change or discouraging thoughts pop in your head - grab your achievement target and read it to yourself.

Take a few deep breaths and then re-read it. In that moment, know that you have what it takes to carry on.

Now write your triggers on a separate piece of paper. We want you to read this out loud to yourself three times in the morning and three times just before bed every day. These are going to be part of your daily routine.

Give yourself at least a few days before starting the next module, repeating your triggers every day.

Junilda Wright

Modules two & three:
R for Release and I for Invite

Junilda Wright

RELEASE & INVITE

The release and invite steps are inextricably linked and therefore we work through both in this module. We hope you have given yourself at least a few days before starting this chapter. And have been repeating your triggers daily as the way to start the process of creating shifts in your mindset.

It is important to go at the pace we recommend, giving yourself time to adjust and make long-lasting transformational changes, rather than chasing a quick fix which ultimately won't last.

Okay, so, we have started to explore your current story and during that process you will have identified some of the thoughts, feelings and emotions that are not serving you.

In this module we are going to start to release these to make room for the good stuff, take back control and to invite new ways of thinking and responding. This is our way of helping you to reframe situations to be more supportive of your mental wellbeing.

We like to think of our thoughts, feelings and emotions as a bubble of energy that surrounds us. All incoming information must go through the bubble before we receive it into our conscious brain, and it therefore will influence how we interpret that information. Likewise, all outgoing information must pass through the bubble, determining our response.

As we described earlier, our energy bubbles are made up of both positive, uplifting energy that makes you feel great inside and out, and of negative, disempowering energy that can make you feel low, stressed or anxious.

The positive energy quickly buzzes through and around you, allowing you to feel vibrant, alert, confident, resilient, at ease with who you are and capable of anything. This is the energy you want to hold on to. The energy you are going to invite more of, to expand and to propel you towards overcoming stress, negativity, anxiety, or low mood.

Conversely, disempowering energy slows you down, it manifests as negative chatter in your head, as anxious thoughts, it undermines your self-confidence. This is the negative energy that we are going to be working to release. It can make you feel tired, unhappy, worried, stressed, doubtful or overly self-critical.

We often don't associate negative thoughts as being something we do to ourselves. Instead, they manifest as focusing on people around us, comparing ourselves to others, escalating everyday issues into bigger problems or catastrophising.

Your energy is created and stored based upon your individual life events. Every word, action or deed you have experienced since the day you were born, will have been linked to an emotion – good or bad – and stored in your subconscious mind as a reference for you to interpret and respond to your world. These form the basis of the core values and beliefs you hold about yourself. Think of these as your life story.

Through our work we have come to see that most of us are living our life based on a story of who we have been told to be, not who we truly are, thus creating many limiting self-beliefs. These thoughts, feelings and emotions can hold you back from feeling your best, cause self-sabotage, anxiety, stress, negative thinking, doubt and/or fear.

It's Just Head Hoo-Ha

One universal way we perpetuate disempowering thoughts is through how we talk to and think of ourselves. Repeatedly saying things like "I'm an idiot" if you don't do something very well, will encourage your subconscious brain into believing it, so here is a mini challenge...

Listen to the voice in your head, every time you think something negative about yourself. Notice how often you do this in a day and see if you can reframe it with more positive, and less self-deprecating words.

We are going to help you to let go of those limiting self-beliefs and release your negative chatter, so you are not stuck in the past or repeating patterns of negative thought and behaviour. Instead, you will increase your emotional vibration. Becoming more you with each day, by inviting how you want to think, feel and behave.

We look at the role other people may play in your current story. To identify where parents, partners or friends have assumed or told you how to be in life. Where they have projected their expectations or view of themselves or others onto you, with comments like: *"Oh, you are just like your grandad, he couldn't handle money either".*

We cannot change other people, so we will be sharing techniques on how you can take back control to stop reacting and start choosing how you respond.

We take a step back and look at your conditioning – the way you have been brought up, the things your parents, family members, teachers, activity or religious leaders, friends, the media, have said or done – these will all have an influence on what is stored in your subconscious. All the rubbish you tell yourself, came from an external source at some point in your past. It isn't who you are.

We then release what is not serving you and start to reframe your perspective by inviting some alternative patterns of thinking. We also explore the things you do enjoy and want more of in your life.

We bring all the positive thoughts, feelings and emotions you identified together in a powerful, transformational daily affirmation to shift your pattern of thinking.

Think of an affirmation like a gym workout for your mind. You have a current way of thinking. These are well travelled pathways in your brain; reinforced by repetition. You are going to start exercising different thought pathways. At first, these will feel forced, but the more you practice the more your brain will learn and begin to understand that you want to think differently. You are essentially telling your brain how to think rather than following your default responses. With repetition these will become your new pathways.

We end the module with a guided visualisation, this time to help you emotionally engage with what you want to invite through your daily affirmation.

Let go of what you don't want

We are going to guide you through an exercise to release the negative thoughts, feelings, and emotions you described in your current story and begin to start to take back control by inviting a new way of thinking.

We refer to the process we are going to share with you as the ARM of change. Picture the muscular arm emoji, as this technique allows you to take back control and feel emotionally strong. So, what does the acronym ARM stand for?

A is for awareness.

In this first step we bring awareness to the disempowering thoughts you experience. Think back to the mini challenge, how many times a day are you telling yourself something negative? We will guide through how to do this.

R is for release.

Using a very simple technique we will show you how you can start to let go of these thoughts and feelings.

M is for move forward.

Once you have released the thoughts, feelings, and emotions you don't want, we invite those that you DO want. This will allow you to move forward and start to create new ways of thinking.

This technique is building on the exercises we did in the Prepare module. We start by releasing the negative stuff and that can feel a little uncomfortable, but we will quickly move on to invite in more positive thoughts and feelings, so please stick with the exercise to the end. Trust that this will have a positive outcome.

Okay, let's get started. Choose a time when you know you have about an hour and a place, where you feel comfortable and know you will not be disturbed. Download the Prepare workbook or grab some paper or a notepad. Remember you can find all the workbooks on our website at https://direction.academy/prism.

Start by reading through your current story again. Bring awareness to what is going on for you by making a list in your workbook or on paper of all the emotions, thoughts, and feelings you described.

Make sure you pick out and write down all the emotions you included in your current story, even if there is some repetition or you have used different words to describe the same thing.

Pause to make your list before you continue reading.

Now go back over your list and group together those that relate directly to you. In other words, those that do not involve other people or events.

For example: *I feel stressed. I feel under time pressure. Sometimes I feel a bit overwhelmed. I feel tired most of the time.*

We are going to do some releasing, so pick out the first three things on your list and put them into the following release statement:

I let go of x, y, z about (insert your scenario). I release these disempowering thoughts feelings and emotions. I am ready to let them go. Repeat 3 times.

It's Just Head Hoo-Ha

Make sure to include a brief description of the scenario this relates to – at work, in social situations, travelling or whatever it is for you, so that your brain can make the connection between your emotional response and the context for that response.

For example: *'I let go of feeling stressed at work, feeling under time pressure, feeling overwhelmed. I release these disempowering thoughts feelings and emotions. I am ready to let them go'.*

Go ahead and create your first release statement.

Once you have your release statement, close your eyes. Take a deep breath in and out. Relax your shoulders. Imagine you are stood in front of another version of yourself. This person is telling you what to do and you are willing to take their words onboard.

Open your eyes, say your release message out loud three times, imagining it is this other version of you telling your energy what to do.

Okay, great. Now you may feel your energy has dropped or you may feel a little weighed down. Bear with us. We are now going to help you lift yourself out of that and to feel more positive and in control.

You have just started to release some of what you no longer want. Now you are going to move forward by inviting in what you do want; So, read through your list and for every item you have on there, write down the opposite. In other words, switch out the disempowering thoughts, feelings and emotions for ones that serve you.

Refer to what you wrote in your replacement story as this may help you find the positive language.

For example: '*I feel stressed* becomes *I feel relaxed and calm*. *I feel under pressure* becomes *I have the time I need...*'and so on.

Remember to watch your language. Just as suggested in the exercises in the Prepare module, avoid any double negatives or just creating a list of what you don't want.

For example, don't include sentences like: '*I don't want to feel stressed. I don't want to feel under time pressure*'.

Remember, this little act of trickery re-wires that sub-conscious brain of yours.
Go ahead and create your new list. You may find it useful to refer to the list of positive words you can find in the Release and Invite workbook.
Great. As in the release exercise, we would like you to take the first three items on your list and use them to invite what you DO want using the sentence below:

'*I allow myself to be / feel / know / believe x,y,z about (insert your scenario). I feel at peace. I allow myself to move forward*'.

Again, make sure to include a brief description of the scenario this relates to – at work, in social situations, travelling or whatever it is for you - so that your brain can make the connection between your emotional response and the context for that response.

For example: '*I allow myself to feel relaxed and calm at work, to know I always have enough time to be in control of my day. I feel at peace. I allow myself to move forward*'.
Again, imagine the other version of you is telling your energy how you to be.
Go ahead and invite in the good stuff. Make it personal to you so you recognise the words you are saying as your own. Repeat your invite statement three times out loud.
Now over the next week or so, go through and repeat this process until you have released and invited everything on your

list. Really emotionally engage with the invite words you use. Visualise having the qualities you are inviting in the present.

Make sure that whatever you release, you then invite the positive directly after, there should be no time-lapse between releasing and inviting. So, for example you may decide to focus on items 1 to 6 in your list today. That's okay - but do both the release and invite for all 6.

With this technique it is important to be realistic. No doubt you have experienced anxiety for some time and in certain situations it has become your default response. It is going to take time to re-wire your brain and think differently.

Therefore, do not become disheartened or too hard on yourself if results are not as quick as expected. As in all things to do with both mind and body, patience and progress are key.

As good nutrition is the long-term lifestyle choice for physical health, equally these techniques are adaptations that once adopted, over time, help create a healthier mindset. Quick fixes rarely work for physical and mental well-being.

Go steady and just focus on a few items on your list each day, knowing that each time you tell yourself how you want to think and feel your brain will pay a little bit more attention. This is you re-writing your story and like any good book it takes time to write.

In the next chapter, we are going to look at how you can release thoughts, feelings and emotions that involve other people.

Junilda Wright

Other People's Impact

We are going to look at how to release negative thoughts, feelings and emotions related to somebody else. This could be something people have said or done that you perceive as a 'wrongdoing' against you or, about how you believe your behaviour is impacting others.

for Awareness.

Most of the time what we say or do has very little really to do with the other person. We all respond to the world based on our own experience of it. Nothing is intrinsically 'good' or 'bad'. Everything gets meaning from what we assign to it, which is based on what we have been taught to believe and our individual life experiences.

Take marriage as an example. If a friend told you they found out their husband had another wife, most likely you would be shocked and angry on their behalf because in western culture we have monogamous relationships. However, the same conversation in Gambia for example, where polygamy is accepted, would elicit a different response.

So, it is our memories, cultural and social conditioning that dictates how we 'hear' or 'experience' every situation and in turn, this will influence how we then respond. Knowing this can be powerful in shaping our relationships.

If someone says or does something mean to us (or us to them) it will be triggered by an unconscious response to something that has occurred within life experience.

A good example of how our subconscious influences us, is to look at what happens when we get angry or cross. When this happens, it will be a response to one of three things:

One – fear or insecurity.

Two – seeing the other as a mirror of something in ourselves that we do not like.

Three – seeing or hearing something that is contrary or alien to our own belief system.

One: Fear or insecurity.

So, the first trigger we mentioned was fear. You may think that fear is too strong a word, or you can't relate to how this could be true, so let's explore this further.

There are all sorts of fears and each one can and does have varying degrees of intensity. There is the fear of failure, of missing out, of being abandoned or rejected, of not being liked, of looking silly or stupid, of not being loved, appearing weak, of uncertainty, of conflict, of being physically or emotionally hurt. And we're sure our list is not exhaustive.

These fears lie in our subconscious brain and so the person experiencing one of these fears doesn't consciously think "Ooh I am worried they won't like me" for instance. Instead, they react in this example with anger. That is their 'go to' response when feeling threatened.

If things escalate into an argument both parties become triggered and their subconscious insecurities will kick in with the original topic of discord often being abandoned, as their fears take over.

Things like the need to not look foolish – often described by the person on the receiving end as 'They always need to be right'.

The need to feel loved and respected, expressed as accusations of not being cared for or even infidelity.

The need to feel valued and good enough, expressed as a list of all the things they bring to the relationship and most likely, a list of the other person's shortcomings.

This fear-based response and not liking what we see in ourselves and/or in others are linked, as there is an element of fear in this response too.

Two: Seeing oneself reflected in others' behaviours.

We all have bits of ourselves we are do not like, maybe are even ashamed of. Things we try to hide.

Therefore, when somebody else demonstrates that behaviour, we worry about being exposed or that somehow, we will betray ourselves. Again, this is all subconscious and rather than acknowledging what is really happening we express it as anger.

Three: Our internal Belief System

The last reason is when someone else's behaviour rubs up against our internal belief system.

Take a parent reprimanding a child who has been naughty. Arguably it is a parent's responsibility to guide their children in the right way to behave. The words they use, the chosen punishment, the perceived severity of the misdemeanour will all be decided based on their individual core beliefs developed from past experiences.

For example, if answering back to a grown-up was something you were severely punished for, you may either follow this in your parenting style as you have stored this as a core belief 'that children do not answer back' or if you feel this adversely affected you, you may believe it is important to be more tolerant.

Whichever, applies, in the moment, whilst reprimanding the child you are doing so based on your own experiences and beliefs.

We want to come back to a point we made earlier about people's 'go to' response; we all have a certain way of behaving when we feel under threat in some way. We don't mean a life-threatening situation, just any situation where one of our fears kicks in. Being worried about missing out or looking stupid for example. Although we respond differently to different situations, we all have one more dominant way of responding, that we go to.

These are what Psychologist Carl Jung, called Shadow Archetypes. In other words, a certain pattern of behaviour we go to unconsciously, that includes traits we consider to be negative and usually keep hidden for fear of recrimination or judgement.

There are lots of interpretations of Jung's different 'Shadow Archetypes', but we find the way James Redfield describes them in his book 'The Celestine Prophecy' easy to relate to.

The intimidator – somebody who uses intimidation to get attention. This could be shouting, aggression, maybe even physical violence. Negative attention that holds you in a pattern of pushing people away before they can disappoint you.

The Interrogator – somebody who is aggressive, not in the way the intimidator displays it, but through lots of questioning and judgemental conversations. Basically, someone who runs down your ideas and dreams, holding you in a seesaw pattern of comparing yourself to others.

The Aloof – somebody who is distant or withholds from engaging with others, including not sharing information. Probably the most common archetype, expressed as passive aggressive behaviours and becoming isolated from true connection with others.

The Poor me – somebody who takes the role of victim, describing they 'bad' experiences, trying to make the other person feel sorry for them and want to help them. This is the most deeply felt and hardest to shift of the archetypes. The energy of sympathy can be as strong as an addiction.

There are nuances to these four broad types, but a person will 'go to' one of these four when under threat. Most people are oblivious to the patterns they run. But through self-authority and ownership of yourself, you can identify when you are falling into any of these 'go to' behaviours and make a conscious decision to change.

We would like you to think of a scenario where someone has had a negative impact on you. if your current story included someone like this, use them for this exercise. If not, think of someone who fits the bill from past experience.

Think about which of the four archetypes they were displaying. It may be that they started as one and then moved to another. For example, they may have started as a 'poor me' and then moved to 'intimidator'.

Thinking about your interactions with this person, the type of things they were saying, the context of the scenario, where do you feel they were coming from? In other words, what type of fear do you believe may have triggered for them?

There's no right or wrong here. This is just about bringing some understanding to how people present certain behaviour which can negatively impact us but when we dig a little deeper, we can see they are being influenced by their subconscious.

Now think about your own behaviour and the role you took. Was it a role you recognise as usually taking in this kind of scenario?

Did you feel triggered? Other than the direct response to the other person, where would you say these feelings came from? Have a think about the different types of fear and whether any of these resonate with you. We will explore this in more detail later in the book.

What we have shared does not excuse or condone ours or others' actions or words, but it can help us understand why we react the way we do and allow us to step back from it. This is just an exercise in observing both our own and others' behaviour and where it might come from. It is not an opportunity to lay blame or label anyone as wrong. Every person has a reason for their behaviour.

Invariably we feel upset, hurt, disappointed, ashamed, guilty, frustrated, resentful or angry in response to what we perceive as 'wrong doings' directed at us. These are very human responses. We are not suggesting that we should not feel this way, as it is unhealthy to deny our feelings, but by stepping back and allowing the person to be who they are, you take back control.

There is a myriad of reasons why someone would want to get a specific negative response from another person, that almost always belies what they are feeling inside and most likely has little to do with what the other person has done or said. Think about bullying and the reasons why someone bullies another. The vicious words and maybe even violence inflicted on another person, all used as a hideous way to falsely lift themselves up.

Allowing others to be who they are, is acknowledging that their behaviour is possibly being influenced by their subconscious and may not just be a reaction to something you did or said. This should just be a point of reflection; it should not lead to you 'taking the blame' or somehow feeling responsible.

It is also good to reflect on your own response. Why did you feel this way? What did the other person's behaviour spark within you? Are you assigning more meaning to the situation because of your beliefs or experiences?

This can help you to feel more in control rather than like a victim or recipient of negativity. You can begin to understand where behaviours are possibly coming from which allows you to let things go more quickly and to release any feelings of guilt, shame, anger or resentment. Emotional maturity is the ability to reflect on others behaviour as well as our own to not be so impacted by these behaviours.

R for Release

So, let's do a release exercise. Grab some paper or Release & Invite workbook. Thinking back to the person in your story or someone who has had a negative impact on you, write down what the person (or group of people) said or did.

Put this into the following sentence:

It's Just Head Hoo-Ha

'I let go of so and so saying x, y, z about (insert your scenario). I release this. I am ready to let this go. I allow them to be who they are'. Repeat this 3 to times to yourself.

Let's say for example a friend had said nasty things about you being stressed every time you meet socially, your release sentence could go something like:

'I let go of my friend saying I am a stress monster every time we meet up. I release this. I am ready to let this go. I allow them to be who they are. I am in control of my reactions and their opinion or projection is not mine'.

Go ahead and create your release statement or if needed, multiple statements.

M for Move forward

The invite process is a little different to what we have done so far. As we have discussed you cannot change the other person or people involved, so we are going to find it in our hearts to forgive them for what they did or said. And to send them unconditional love.

We know this may be difficult as your emotional wound may be deep, but we really encourage you to say the words even if you are not feeling it right now. We are not asking you to condone what they did, just to forgive them. The only way to truly release yourself is to forgive.

'I accept that (person) has hurt me, I accept that they have their own opinion, I am ready to let this go and move forward, I forgive (person) to allow myself to feel at peace'.

'I release myself from you and you are released from me'.

'I allow myself to move forward'.
Repeat 3 times.

When we talk about forgiving someone who has hurt you, this isn't in anyway about letting them do it again! Most people think that's what forgiveness is. To forgive someone is to stop holding on to that hurt or anger, as eventually it turns into bitterness. It sets you free as that person no longer gets to hold you in a pattern of hurt or anger.

So go ahead and invite forgiveness and love.

We know this may have been challenging for you. You may feel you want to repeat the release and invite statements over the coming days or weeks until you feel you have shifted the thoughts, feelings and emotions around this. Take your time with this and the shifts will happen.

Have a think about which of the four archetypes best describes you and which of the fears pop up for you. It's always good to understand where you are coming from.

In the next chapter we look at how we release thoughts, feelings, and emotions and about how you believe you impact others.

Your Impact on Others

We are going to explore how to release our thoughts, feelings and emotions related to how we believe we influence other people or how we think they perceive us.

If you included other people in your current story, use them for this exercise. If not, think about a person or group of people where you feel concerned you are adversely impacting the relationship, or you believe they have a negative perception of you. If you feel this does not apply to you, that is great, you can skip this exercise. Please don't start to question your relationships too much, trust your initial instinct that they are good.

It is difficult to be objective when it comes to beliefs about how we believe other people perceive us. Most of us have a false impression of how we believe we are seen by others. So, the first thing we would like you to do, is to write down what you believe to be the other person's or group's perception of you.

Start with whatever you wrote in your current story, if you have something, otherwise, think of somebody this applies to.

For example: '*I feel my boss thinks I am not doing my job well and that I take too long to get things done*'.

Go over what you have written again to see if any additional thoughts, feelings or emotions come up for you. Add some description about the scenario.

For example: '*I am sure my boss values my colleagues more than me. They always seem to get their reports finished before me. They all laugh and joke together. I am sure they think I am boring*'.

Try and go into as much detail as you can.

Once you feel you have captured everything, we want you to ask yourself what evidence supports your view. Only include it if the person / group said something directly to you.

For example: '*My boss said I am always late handing in my monthly reports*'.

Do not include other people's anecdotal comments as these will be coming from their perception of the relationship, which as we previously discussed will be influenced by the beliefs they have stored in their subconscious. And who knows what's going on for them!

Therefore, don't include comments like: '*My colleague said my boss told her he gives her the reports to do as she gets them done quickly*'.

There are two possible outcomes here:

One, you have no real evidence to support your belief, in which case ask yourself what has led you to believe this? Did someone else plant the thought in your head, or have you assumed this to be the case? Both are very typical.

If it is you making assumptions, know that you are being influenced by your own limiting self-beliefs. Never forget how

It's Just Head Hoo-Ha

unsupportive your inner voice can be! Either way, take back control by releasing these thoughts, feelings, and emotions.

We will guide you through how to release this in just a moment.

Two, the person did say something directly to you to let you know how they feel about your relationship. In this case, again you can take back control.

In the prepare module you described what you want your new way of thinking and behaving to be. Working through these exercises and changing your mindset to make this a reality will allow you to start to impact your relationships.

If someone has accused you of being distant, late, angry, stressed or whatever it is they said to you; know that you can positively change your interactions with them.

Regardless of where your belief about someone's perception of you comes from, we are going to release this belief, as this does not serve you. Use what you wrote about the relationship to create your release statement.

I let go of x, y, z about (insert your scenario). I release these disempowering thoughts, feelings and emotions. I am ready to let them go.

Repeat 3 times.

For example: '*I let go of feeling my boss does not value me and the feeling that they do not think I am good at my job, by taking too long to finish my work. I release these disempowering thoughts, feelings and emotions. I am ready to let them go*'.

Write and say your release statement.
As before, we are going invite what you DO want.

For each disempowering statement, you are going to write a new statement, using positive language. As we have discussed, we cannot change other people – and in this case, we do not even know what other people really think or believe.

We can only take control of our own thoughts. So, we want you to describe how you want to feel about the scenario for example:

'I allow myself to believe I add value at work, that I finish my work on time, that I am good at what I do and that I am fun to work with. I feel at peace. I allow myself to move forward'.

Go ahead and create your new way of seeing this scenario using the sentence below.

'I allow myself to be /feel / know / believe x,y,z about (insert your scenario). I feel at peace. I allow myself to move forward'.

Repeat 3 times.

Your Timeline

In this exercise you are going to create a timeline. This very practical approach allows you to see the memories you are holding and where the foundation for your self-beliefs has originated. From there you can release what is not serving you, remember good times, and explore the 'feel good' things you would like to experience and have more of in your life.

Dr Athena Staik describes this method as "a tool to make conscious self-directed changes that, rewire your brain to heal itself. Known as plasticity, your brain has an innate capacity to make changes in positive, healing directions."

Again, your timeline is personal to you but no matter what this looks like you will:

- See certain patterns of thinking or responses across different events
- Understand how your past experiences have shaped the way you respond to life events today and how you can start to change your patterns of thinking
- Find new, more positive ways of interpreting past events to allow you to think differently about things that are happening to you now and in the future

- Identify positive aspects of your life that empower you and you can invite more of to grow your confidence, resilience, and happy feelings

Ultimately, this exercise is to help identify disempowering thoughts and limiting self-beliefs, so that you can release them to make room for new, more positive ways of thinking. It will also highlight the positive aspects of your life and help you to look for ways to invite more of these.

Make sure you have at least 40 minutes of uninterrupted time to complete the first part of this exercise. Print out the Release and Invite workbook you can find on our website https://direction.academy/prism or take a fresh sheet of paper and mark it up the same way as shown in the workbook.

Note down a list of your significant life events. Include both positive and negative situations.

When considering your timeline, think of any experiences that impacted your life, any emotions that affected you, both positively and negatively. There are the more obvious ones, such as marriage, divorce, birth and death. However, it could equally be an event you experienced or were witness to or even hurtful words that you often replay in your mind. Overall, the timeline will highlight anything that is significant and personal to you and your story. Allow your mind the freedom to goes where it wants to, including travelling back to your childhood days. Take as long as you need to write your list.

Make sure you have completed your timeline before you move on and read the next chapter, where we will be reviewing the events you have identified.

Release the Negative

If you have not completed the exercise from the previous chapter, please go back and do that before starting this one.

We are going to look at the events you put on the negative side of your timeline. We will explore how your past events may be influencing your life and identify limiting beliefs that need to be released.

We will review the events you plotted on the positive side of your timeline in a later chapter and which of those experiences or responses you may decide you want to invite more of.

This exercise can be quite emotional. We ask that you trust the process and know that you will feel the benefit of releasing the negative, limiting beliefs you have been carrying around for years.

It is important to take your time and go at the pace we set. If you try to rush or work through too many things at one time you are likely to feel overwhelmed. You can always pause and take some deep breaths to calm your mind and regain focus.

Let us begin. Go back through the events you listed on your timeline and write down what made each one a negative situation for you.

What were you feeling at the time? Try and recall.

If someone else was involved, what did they say or do to evoke the negative emotion in you? Did you Respond? How?

For example: '*My best friend told me my thighs are fat. I felt hurt by what my friend said. I felt she was being cruel as I believe she knew I would be upset. I felt ashamed of the way my legs look. I wanted to cover up my legs*'.

Or '*I remember going for a walk with my dog after my Dad had shouted at me. I felt I had not done anything wrong. He often shouted for no good reason. I felt scared and lonely. I felt as though my dog was the only one who loved me. Mum never defended me. She just let Dad shout. I felt alone*'.

Now we are going to complete the table in your workbook. Recreate the table on a sheet of paper if you can't print it out.

We would like you to read the questions below and put a tick against each one that applies to the first event you described. If a question is not applicable that's okay, just ignore it.

Ask yourself if you were trying to fulfil someone else's expectations at the time?

Did you feel you needed to be or do something because you felt that was what someone else expected from you?

Did you feel you had let someone down?

Were you seeking somebody else's approval or validation? Or trying to please someone?

Did you want someone to acknowledge that you had said or done the right thing?

Was there something you were trying to avoid happening?

Was there something you were worried would happen if you did or did not say or do something?

Were you afraid you would fail?

Did you feel useless?

Did you feel unsafe or threatened?

Did you feel scared?

It's Just Head Hoo-Ha

Were you afraid you would be judged? Note, this is a different to seeking validation or approval. As you want to avoid judgement, whereas when we seek approval, we are inviting the other person – often unconsciously - to pass judgement on our actions.

Did you feel somehow you were not worthy? Or did you believe you were not good enough?

Did you feel abandoned, hurt, lonely or unloved?

Did you feel angry or frustrated?

Did you feel resentful?

Did you feel ashamed or embarrassed?

Were you worried about looking stupid or being made fun of?

Did you feel sad, unhappy, or depressed?

Did you feel Inferior, insignificant, or taken advantage of?

Did you feel unattractive, ugly, or fat?

Did you feel trapped, helpless, or powerless?

Now, go through and tick off the same questions for all the events you have listed on the negative side of your timeline. Take your time to do this thoroughly.

Have a look at which questions you put ticks against. Are there any with multiple ticks? This shows you where there are patterns in the way you felt and thought about events. Now you are aware of what is going on in your subconscious, you are going to release these negative memories and invite a positive mindset.

So, as before we would like you to take the first three questions you ticked in the table and put the associated thoughts and feelings into the following release statement: then say it out loud:

'I let go of x, y, z. I release these disempowering thoughts feelings and emotions. I am ready to let them go'.

Repeat 3 times.

For example: '*I let go of seeking other people's approval, of trying to please other people and fearing failure. I release these disempowering thoughts feelings and emotions. I am ready to let them go*'.

You have brought awareness to what was going on for you and released it, now you are going to invite a new way of thinking about the past. This will start to positively influence how you respond in the future. It will create a significant shift in your thinking as what is stored in our subconscious brain determines how we receive information and respond to it.

Like the release exercise, we want you to take the first three questions you ticked and turn them into a positive statement to invite what you want. Refer to the table below to complete this sentence:

I allow myself to be /feel / know / believe x,y,z. I feel at peace. I allow myself to move forward. Repeat 3 times.

Feel free to add your own words but remember, do not write, and say what you don't want. Instead, positively state what you *do* want. For example

I allow myself to know I am enough, to feel relaxed about the future and to know I am good at what I do. I feel at peace. I allow myself to move forward.

Go ahead and invite in the good stuff.

Thoughts, feelings & emotions	New way of thinking
Trying to fulfil expectations	I am enough
Seeking validation, approval, trying to please	I validate myself. I make my own decisions
Worried about outcome, anxious	I am relaxed about the future

Fear of failure, useless	I succeed. I am good at what I do
Unsafe, threatened, scared	I feel safe and secure
Fear of being Judged	I feel confident. I like who I am
Not worthy, not good enough	I am worthy. I am good enough
Abandoned, hurt, lonely, left out, not wanted or unloved	I feel included. I feel cared for. I feel loved
Angry, frustrated	I feel calm. I feel in control
Resentful	I am happy
Ashamed, embarrassed, looking stupid, made fun of	I am confident. I like myself
Sad, unhappy, depressed	I am happy. I feel good
Inferior, insignificant, taken advantage of	I am important. I feel valued. I am appreciated
Unattractive, ugly, fat	I am attractive. I look great
Trapped, powerless	I feel free to do what I want. I am in control
Misunderstood, unfairly treated	I feel understood. I am treated well
At fault, to blame, done something wrong	I am okay. I am free

Repeat this process until you have released everything you put a tick against. It is important to take your time to do this. If you want to, you can do some now and then come back to it as many times as needed to finish the exercise. You don't need to do this in one go but remember to always do the invite for everything you release.

Allow yourself to emotionally engage with this if you can, but don't worry if you aren't feeling it, just keep going and trust that over time, with repetition you will start to.

A key thing to remember is that we cannot change the past. We can only change the future. So, don't dwell on what has happened. Celebrate how strong you have been to get through what life has thrown in your path and know that you are starting to make changes.

You may like to add another sentence or two to your daily affirmations if something has come up for you that you would like to invite more of. We expect your affirmation list to be a constantly evolving thing as you too evolve.

We have recorded a very powerful guided session to help you release old thought patterns and welcome in the new. Head over to https://direction.academy/prism to listen to it.

It's Just Head Hoo-Ha

Invite the Good Stuff

We have focused on the events you plotted on the negative side of your timeline. In this chapter we are going to look at your positive events. This is a lovely way to remind ourselves of fun and happy times as often we can get weighed down with what hasn't gone well and forget the good stuff.

We are going to remember what it feels like to be happy, confident, calm, relaxed – all the positive, empowering emotions – and to see what it was that made you feel that way. Grab your notebook or workbook and let's begin.

We would like you to read through all the positive events you listed on your timeline and make a note of what thoughts, feelings and emotions these bring up for you. If, whilst doing this, a new event comes to mind and you would like to add it to your timeline, feel free to do so. The more positivity you can muster, the better.

For example: *I felt happy and carefree. I felt confident and strong. I felt safe and loved.*
And what made these events good?

I was with my friends. We always had a laugh together or I was painting. I love painting.

We were moving into our new home and life felt full of possibilities.

I had a great day at work where everything came together. I had a strong sense of accomplishment.

Go ahead and do this now.

Now you have a list of positive emotions, let's invite more of them in.

Read the following sentence out loud:

I am ready to release any resistance to feeling good.

I am ready to feel a,b,c,d,e, - go ahead and say all the positive emotions you have listed. List them all and anything else that comes to mind, even if it is repetition.

Smile to yourself and then repeat these 2 more times, adding to your list of feel-good feelings each time.

Don't worry if you are not feeling as great as maybe you would like. Just know that you are making small, incremental changes to your thought patterns with every exercise you complete. This will gather intensity with repetition.

We are going to create a new daily affirmation in the next chapter bringing together all the 'invite' statements which will bring some great energy and momentum to this.

For now, though, we would like you to look at what you wrote down as the reasons for why you felt good. Are any of these things you would like to start doing again? Like a hobby, socialising with friends, a sporting activity, travel, study, anything?

If nothing jumps out at you from your list, ask yourself what *new* thing do you feel inspired to try? We really want you to find something, no matter how small. Don't allow obstacles or excuses to get in your way. This is just your brain reacting to the

It's Just Head Hoo-Ha

possibility of change. Recognise this for what it is and re-focus your attention on deciding on an activity.

If you are drawing a blank on this, take yourself somewhere different with the sole purpose of finding inspiration. A change of scenery helps to open our minds to new perspectives.

Use the internet to look up short courses or explore new careers. Talk to different people about their interests.

Move the furniture in your house around if you can. We used to think Feng Shui meant tidy up a bit, but there is a heap of scientific proof that your living space really affects your mindset and ability to be inspired.

This may be starting to trigger your overwhelm buttons, so let's talk this through to find a way to make this possible for you. Start with something small for now, like joining a yoga class or going for a walk once a week, knitting or cooking.

Ask a friend, colleague, or family member if they will come with you if it involves going somewhere outside of your home. If joining an activity with others feels too daunting now, look to see if you can find a video on the internet that you could follow at home. Always remember, no one walks out the door brimming with confidence without taking those first shaky steps. Confidence is acquired through experience.

If your negative chatter continues to present you with reasons why you cannot do this, use the techniques we have just learnt to release it. For example:

I release feeling I cannot do a Judo class because I do not have time.
I know I have time to do a Judo class.

And then look for ways you can make it a reality. Swapping commitments around. Ask a family member or friend to watch the kids for a couple of hours, follow along to Judo videos at home. It is possible if you believe it is.

This exercise is about having more fun and doing things you enjoy, but it is also about building up your resilience. By finding solutions to perceived blockers, you are taking back control. Once you have pushed through and done what you want to do, it always feels good. Enjoy the process.

It's Just Head Hoo-Ha

New Neural Pathways

We have done a lot of releasing and inviting new ways of thinking. You may already be feeling shifts in the way you feel, which is great. If not, don't worry that is fine, just trust that this *is* happening for you. Whatever you do, be sure to dismiss the negative voice in your head if it starts, the voice that may be telling you to give up, that this is not working, what's the point? Nothing has changed. These kinds of thoughts are very typical.

Our brain works by finding patterns and any changes to the established pathways are initially treated as outliers and are rejected or explained away even when the change will positively impact us.

Our brain will try to sabotage our efforts, presenting us with arguments about why we should stop and stay, or go back to, how we were. The arguments reflect our limiting beliefs about ourselves and therefore can be very convincing. Recognise this may be happening and smile to yourself. It is a sign that you are successful, and that change is taking place. Your brain wouldn't react if nothing was going on.

Another way this can play out is you start to feel a change and feel great, but then after a week or so, have a setback - a bad day at work, an argument or something similar, and your brain will jump back into the negative mindset. You need to remember the negative pathways will remain with you for a long time and you will most likely fall into them again at some point, everybody does.

If so, simply recognise what has happened and carefully restart the positive thought patterns. Over time it will become easier to switch back and the old negative thought patterns will become more alien and easier to reject.

What we are going to do in this chapter will help to propel you forward. Closer to achieving the goal you described in the Prepare module. We are going to create a new, even more powerful trigger statement bringing together all the thoughts, feelings and emotions you identified in each of the invite exercises. Remember, essentially what your affirmations will be doing is rewiring your brain. You are giving your brain instructions on how you want to think and feel. By repeating these instructions again and again you start to etch this neural pathway into your mind, gradually erasing your default unsupportive thoughts and feelings.

So, we would like you to go through all your invite statements from the previous exercises and write down in your workbook or in your notebook all the positive thoughts, feelings, and emotions you invited.

For example:

I feel happy and calm in social situations, I feel content, I am good at my job, I have enough time to do what I need to etc.

Go ahead and create your list.

You should have a lovely long list of positivity. Just stop a moment and allow yourself to take this in. What you have written down in front of you is your new reality. This is how you are going to think, feel, behave and respond. Wow! Amazing!

Now, we want you to craft 3 or 4 sentences using the thoughts, feelings, and emotions you have on your list. As always, watch your language. Make sure you use positive, empowering words and avoid double negatives.

Also, use the present tense, imagine this is already happening for you. This is important as you are telling your brain this is how I think, feel and respond now. Not how you are going to think, feel and respond in the future. Start to make this your reality right now.

To reinforce this, we want you to prefix your affirmation with 'today'. This is important as it's quite common for us to start to second guess the future – this may happen and that may happen, which can lead to overwhelm. To minimise these feelings just take each day as it comes. For example:

Today, I am good at my job. I am a valued member of the team. Today, I make my own decisions. Today, I feel confident and in control. Today, I feel relaxed and calm. Today I look after my own needs.

You can add more to your statement if you feel you want to, but don't make it so long that you struggle to remember it.

We want you to start saying these affirming sentences to yourself every morning repeating it three times and the same again in the evening. It's no problem if you say it slightly differently each time or if you feel the desire to add extra bits that day – it's all good.

Don't worry if you are not feeling this way now. Through consistent repetition, you will notice a shift in your thinking which will in turn impact the way you feel and behave. Remember it is repetition, repetition, repetition that makes the difference. The more you do this, the more your way of thinking will shift.

There is a chance that your brain will try to distract you. It could be that you say two repetitions and then get side-tracked into thinking something else – no problem. Just notice what has happened and bring your attention back to your affirmation.

Likewise, you may decide to say this while brushing your teeth, for example and then realise you forgot to do it one morning. Again, no problem, simply say them as soon as you remember. Don't avoid saying them. You may consider putting something in place that will help you to remember. Say for example you do decide to do your affirmations whilst brushing your teeth, stick a gold star on the bathroom mirror so that every time you see it, you are reminded. The key thing is to keep going and trust that over time this is going to make an enormous positive impact on you.

Be kind to yourself and be patient. Often when we set about making changes, we want, and expect them to happen immediately.

While we do want you to start to feel the changes quickly, you do need to be realistic. Most of us experience gradual, incremental change, rather than a big bang type of shift. To experience sustainable, long-lasting changes to your mindset it's going to take three to four weeks.

Give yourself the time and space to allow this to happen following the techniques we have shared. Try to avoid thoughts like "I don't want to feel this way". "I don't want to feel unhappy anymore. I should be feeling better" As much as you desperately want to make the change, the more you engage with this kind of thinking the more you hold yourself in this place. Instead, trust that every day you say your affirmations and engage your new ways of thinking, is a day closer to achieving your goal.

Well done for getting this far. You should be very proud of yourself. Keep going!

Visualisation

In the last chapter you created your daily affirming statements. Please keep going with these every day. If you forget to do them one time, don't worry you can just do them as soon as you remember.

In the Prepare module we talked about how important it is to emotionally engage when we are looking to make changes in our lives. If we don't build up some positive feelings about what we want to achieve, the chances are, we eventually give up and revert to our old habits and patterns of thinking. But when something makes us feel good, we naturally want more of that and are therefore more motivated to keep moving forward.

In fact, we release a chemical called dopamine, which is directly linked to motivation, when doing things that feel good. As we all want to feel good, our brain will want to steer us back to things that helped us feel that way.

To take advantage of the way your brain works and really start to feel good about your new way of responding to the world, we are going to do a visualisation.

Well, we are calling it that, but we will guide you through to either 'see' what is going on or to 'feel' what's going on or maybe even both.

You can use this visualisation technique to help prepare for upcoming events that you may feel anxious about: a work dinner, a family party or weekend away - anything.

The technique is all about practicing in advance of an event, how you want to think and feel, so you know how you want to respond and can remind yourself if you start to feel anxious, panicky or feel yourself spiralling into negative thinking. This is more effective than waiting until you are in the scenario, as it is difficult to think of strategies in the moment, especially if your amygdala - the part of our brain that initiates the 'fight or flight' response, is engaged and you are starting to feel anxious.

This time we want you to focus on your goal. The scenario you described in your replacement story.

Start this when you have time and can find a comfortable place to relax without being interrupted for **at least 20 minutes**. You can sit or lie down, whichever you prefer.

We recommend playing the recording of this session which you can find on our website at https://direction.academy/prism.

If you do not have access to the internet, you can read through the process. Take your time, pausing as you go to imagine and feel the images we suggest.

Get comfortable, maybe grab a blanket to snuggle under, have a little wriggle around. Take a nice deep breath in through your nose and out through your mouth. Breathe in, feel your ribcage expand as you fill your lungs. If you can, hold the breath for a few moments and then slowly release it through your mouth.

And again, breathe in and as you do imagine breathing in positivity, love and happiness and as you breath out you are releasing any thoughts, feelings and emotions that are not serving you. Let these go. Beautiful.

Bring your attention to your head. Move it gently forward toward your chest, back to centre and then gently back and then to the centre. Check you are not frowning or clenching your jaw. Breathe.

Bring your shoulders up to your ears and gently release back down. Relax your back and your stomach muscles. Release any tension around your pelvis. Breathe in and out. Let your legs go. They feel heavy and relaxed. Let go of any tension in your calves and feet. Relax your arms and hands.

Trust that any and everything is possible, at least just for the duration of this visualisation.

We would like you to think about the goal you set in the Prepare module. Remind yourself of what it is you want to achieve. Imagine you have already achieved it.

You feel good. You feel relaxed and calm. You feel confident and capable. You feel in control. You feel happy. Smile. Take a nice deep breath in and out. Smile again. You feel great. You feel at peace.

Say your daily affirmation to yourself. *I am calm and relaxed, I am valued* – whatever this is for you.

Picture yourself somewhere that relates to your goal. Breathe in and out. Remember you feel good. You feel relaxed and calm.

Where are you?

What are you doing? Know that whatever it is *you* are in control.

What can you see?

What things are around you?

What colours can you see?

What kind of day is it?

Breathe in and out. Imagine that relaxed, calm feeling expanding, grower bigger and stronger, more empowering with every breath in. Smile.

Who is with you?

What, if anything, are you saying?

What are they saying?

You feel good. Breathe

What else can you hear in the background? Birds? Music? Laughter? Singing?

Notice how good you are feeling. How happy you are. Smile.

What can you smell? A general fresh, clean smell? Cooking? A perfume? Breathe in and out. Relax.

Breathe in and feel your lungs expand with fresh air. Breathe out. You feel content and happy. You feel strong and capable. Smile.

Every time you say your affirmation, we want you to picture this scene and know that this is your new way of responding.

Let your thoughts drift in and out for a few moments.

It's time now to come back into the room. Keep smiling and gently wiggle your fingers and toes. Start to move a little and now bring your attention fully back into the room.

It's Just Head Hoo-Ha

Junilda Wright

Module four: Shift

Junilda Wright

Sabotage

Congratulations on getting this far! You are ready to start the shift module. Before we describe what we are going to cover in this module, we want to share some advice on how to deal with self-sabotage.

You have your daily affirmations that you are repeating at least every morning and every evening. Keep going with these and trust that over the next few weeks you are going to experience shifts in the way you think, feel, and behave.

While these are busy re-shaping the way you respond, there are some techniques you can use to combat any sabotage attempts your brain may be presenting you with.

You will find that even though you work to release disempowering thoughts, feelings, and emotions, your brain may want to try to sabotage your efforts by keeping you from starting to make the change, convincing you it's not worth continuing or trying to over-turn the success you have already achieved.

So now is a good time to introduce what we call the three As. Awareness, Action, Anyway!

Awareness. If negative or discouraging thoughts pop up – and don't beat yourself up if they do as this is a very common response, the first step is to be aware and to recognise them for what they are. The brain does not like change and will do anything to keep you in your current vibration, doing the same things and using the same brain patterns.

Action. Once you recognise what that brain of yours may be up to, the next step is to continue to take action. Keep taking small steps that will help you to move from how you are currently behaving (your habits) and thinking (beliefs) to how you want to think and act. You will have started to release your old thoughts, feelings and emotions but your brain may present you with some of these same thoughts again, with add-ons like 'Why bother? You didn't succeed last time you tried'. 'You have been anxious for years; you won't be able to stick to this.' 'You are always so tired after work; you won't feel like doing the exercises in the evening' and so on. It's at this point that you could give in, but this is when you really need to stay strong.

Anyway. This is when you need to take action **anyway**, despite what your sabotaging brain may be trying to convince you of. Stay determined. Stay strong and just follow the steps we share with you.

If this has not happened for you yet (and you may be lucky that it never does) we suggest you still read on so you know how to deal with self-sabotage, just in case it does rear its ugly head.

If this is happening for you now, take a moment to write down the arguments your brain has been presenting you with as reasons to stop.

For each argument you have written down, try to find a workable solution that will allow you to take action **anyway**.

Some helpful tips:

Choose a specific day and time to do the exercises in this book. If you don't carve out a specific time you will always be able to find excuses not to do it.

Don't try to do too much. Spend no more than an hour each time, otherwise it will feel too much of a commitment and there will be a high chance you won't do it.

You could ask a trusted friend or family member to help keep you accountable. Let them know what you want to achieve each week and ask them to check-in with you.

Write out your strategies to overcome any self-sabotage attempts.

A simple tool is to use the phrase 'Just for today' before you think or say anything:

"Just for today I will treat myself kindly".
"Just for today I will stay calm and relaxed".
"Just for today I will not assume I'm at fault".

Doing this pulls your focus to today and only today. Anxiety comes from trying to second guess and prepare for all eventualities that haven't even happened yet. The rule of 'Just for today' stops that cycle.

SHIFT

In the previous two modules we have worked on bringing awareness to what is going on for you, started to release these thoughts, feelings and emotions and then invited new ways of thinking to allow you to move forward and positively change the way you respond to the world.

In this module we are going to turn our attention to shifting the behaviours that anxiety, stress, negative thinking, and low mood can manifest as.

We will take three different approaches. In the first group of exercises we will explore very practical techniques to shift your current results and allow you to take back control. We then look at some widely held disempowering self-beliefs and how to remove their influence on you. We end the module by looking at where your anxiety and stress stems from and how to make very powerful shifts in the energy you are holding to let that go and be free from it.

We have deliberately structured the module this way to allow you to feel you are taking back control from the get-go and to build your trust in us and the techniques we share.

It's Just Head Hoo-Ha

Think of this like planning a journey. You know where you are and where you want to get to. Now you need to identify what roadblocks may be in your way, how they got there and most importantly, how to navigate through them. Notice we said 'through' and not 'around'. This is key. It is no good trying to navigate around your anxiety and stress as that would mean the neural pathways that trigger you into these states remain. And if they remain, they could start to creep back in. So, we are going to navigate through.

That means you are going to find ways to replace your existing thoughts and behaviours with others. You are going to *shift* your mindset.

We will share a range of approaches. They are all super simple. There is a high chance at some point you are going to think one of the techniques is silly or ineffective and not want to do it. If this happens consider whose voice is behind these feelings. Question whether it truly is yours.

More likely it is going to be the voice of friends, family or colleagues who are influencing you. When we say 'voice' it won't be that you are directly hearing someone talk to you, it's more of a feeling that somehow others will know what you are doing and will ridicule you.

This is very hard to recognise when it happens as its very deep-seated. It tends to manifest as just an uncomfortable feeling, an unexplained reluctance to want to step forward. It is not something you are likely to have recognised or acknowledged before. So, if you find yourself resisting doing one of the techniques, pause for a moment, take a deep breath and consider your response. Notice what comes to mind in that moment. Who comes to mind. Whether you are concerned someone will ridicule you for doing this. Go with your very first thoughts as these are the truest. As soon as your rational brain kicks in, it will try to convince you otherwise.

Recognising your own voice within this process is very important and literally life changing. It applies not only to performing the techniques in this book, but to anything in life you seek to do. So, from now on, when sabotaging thoughts arise, pause and rather than allow yourself to be swept along with that train of thought, consider whose voice is loudest. Is it genuinely yours or a combination of other people's voices and opinions?

Be careful though. This is a not blame game, another default behaviour we can easily get sucked into. It is not about getting angry or upset with the 'voices'; It is simply acknowledging the root of your resistance. To help to avoid blame, give your sabotaging voice a name. He or she can then represent all the negative voices and opinions and then whenever that feeling or voice pops up you can say 'ah, hi Sally or Steve' or whatever you have named them, as acknowledging their existence helps to diminish their power.

As we move through this module, we will remind you of Sabotaging Sally.

You are going to be developing a written strategy. This will be a list of tools and techniques you feel comfortable committing to using. It is critical that you develop a strategy upfront so that you can refer to it if required. If you leave it and decide to only address your anxiety or negative thinking in the moment, your chances of success are reduced as your attention will be diverted by the emotional and physiological responses that may kick in at the time. So be sure to either copy the coping strategy headings in the example below or download a copy from our website https://direction.academy/prism.

Tool / Technique:	Diaphragmatic Breathing
Scenario:	Using public transport
Use:	To calm my breathing & stop panicky feelings
Practice:	Just before bed

It's Just Head Hoo-Ha

Once you have identified the strategies that work for you, we are going to bring full awareness to your anxiety or negative chatter to allow you to confront it head on. We will explore techniques that allow you to believe you have the skills to handle what is going on for you and ultimately to stop the cycle. We are going to dig down much deeper to expose every single anxious or negative thought, feeling and emotion to eliminate the frequency, intensity and duration of your anxiety or negative thinking. We will guide you through this whole process. Trust that you are ready to do this.

As you start to shift how you think and behave in certain situations you will notice a shift in the way you feel, in your body's physiological-emotional states. These positive feelings lead to greater and more positive shifts in your thinking and behaviour and the cycle continues, lifting you back into feeling calm, relaxed, happy, confident, resilient and content.

These behavioural shifts may feel a little uncomfortable, as any change, regardless of if good or bad, can feel unsettling initially.

Stick with it and trust that you will start to see results quickly as your brain starts to make new neural pathways. Try not to overthink the process, simply follow the exercises and we will guide you through how to make these changes. As with all the amazing work you are doing, be kind to yourself.

Unless we state otherwise, we strongly recommend conquering just one of the exercises a week to give yourself time to adjust.

Plan

In this Shift chapter we are going to talk about how our fears, if left unchecked, can get the better of us and continue to perpetuate anxious or negative thinking. As we discussed at the beginning of the book, all anxiety and negative self-talk stems from a fear of something – fear of what might happen or fear of what has happened before, happening again.

In the following chapters we are going to explore different techniques for overcoming these fears to allow you to take back control and calm your anxious mind and body.

It's good to plan and to be prepared, to try and remove some of the ambiguity from situations, although it is impossible to know the outcome of every scenario. Despite our conscious brain knowing this to be true there are times when we will get caught up trying to second-guess how things are going to turn out.

It would be amazing if we could predict the future, but instead this pattern of thinking can cause overwhelm, worry and anxiety and we can find ourselves entangled in a web of 'what if' scenarios.

We then end up:

Procrastinating - Putting off taking action, giving ourselves any number of plausible excuses: too busy, no money, not the right time.

Sabotaging what we have started, to avoid a perceived bigger failure later.

Spiralling into panic & rumination – repetitive anxious or negative thoughts, where your mind keeps going over the same thing again and again.

Catastrophising – believing, irrationally, that the outcome will be far worse than it is.

Exhibiting low esteem or a lack of confidence which often means we seek reassurance from others that everything will be okay (which, as we will discuss in a later chapter, doesn't always work out as expected)

Seeking perfectionism – not taking action until you are sure that the result will be perfect.

Or maybe a mixture of these. Whichever way our fear manifests is frustrating, disempowering and at times crippling. We close ourselves off to social and work-related interactions, to new and exciting opportunities to grow, explore and have fun.

Invariably, as we have discussed before, these fears are not fully conscious thoughts. It is only when we start to question our behaviour that we can see how the limiting beliefs or old wounds that we have stored in our subconscious, hold us back. There are many reasons why these fears rear up – everybody's story is different, but as the timeline exercise demonstrated, most commonly they stem from childhood experiences where we were criticised, harshly judged, ridiculed, were not emotionally supported, not trusted, felt scared or abandoned or were made to feel a failure.

Where you tried something and it did not go well and instead of shaking it off and trying again or moving on to the next thing, you began to generalise, believing that because you failed at something, you will fail again.

But we can interrupt these patterns of thinking. Any repeated action or thought is seen by our brain as important. It gives more blood and white cells to support this neural pathway. In the same way our brains have stored the negative thought patterns, we can use the same approach to replace these with more uplifting, supportive thinking. Your job is to take back control and show your brain the new way you want to respond. With emotional engagement and repetition your brain will store this new neural pathway as the important one diverting away from the anxiety inducing pattern.

It's important to note that when we describe the possible triggers for your current way of thinking, we are not necessarily talking about traumatic events. For most people experiencing anxiety they would describe their childhood as 'normal'. The triggers are often formed from seemingly harmless events. It will depend on how your younger self, with no real frame of reference to how the world works, decided to interpret the event.

Let's look at some techniques on how you can start to reset the way you think. Let's start with procrastination, self-sabotage and 'what if' thinking. These are behaviours most of us have experienced before, so even if they do not feel like problems for you now, we encourage you to go through the exercise.

Not knowing how things will turn out can lead to anxious or negative thoughts. Therefore, we will show you how you can remove some of the ambiguity by creating a clear action plan and in this way, you take away the worry and rumination.

Grab a piece of paper or download the Shift workbook and let's get started.

For this exercise we would like you to write down something that you want to do but may have been putting off doing or something that you started and then abandoned. Maybe, it's a dream you have held for some time. Maybe you want to start dating again, maybe it is something work-related, like changing your working hours or pushing for promotion, maybe its health

It's Just Head Hoo-Ha

related, like losing weight or starting an exercise class – pick anything that is relevant to you, no matter how big or small.

Firstly, think about what it is you want to achieve. Don't worry about the practicalities of it. For now, just go ahead and write it down.

Ask yourself how your life would be enriched if you achieved your goal. Now think about how your life would be enriched even if you were only partially successful in achieving your goal.

What lessons could you learn from trying? What benefits are there? Keep things positive.

These don't need to be huge, life-changing things. Anything that brings happiness and fun into your life is worth doing. Let's say you want to start going to a yoga class for example. This would increase your flexibility, help to alleviate the pain in your back and allow you to meet new people.

Now thinking about your goal, break this down into smaller goals or steps to allow you to achieve it – the smaller the better to allow you to take just one step at a time. Write these down.

For example: I want to join a yoga class. I could break this down into finding out where yoga classes are being held. Reading reviews of this particular yoga practice online. Looking on Google maps on how to get to the class. Giving the yoga teacher a call to see if there are spaces. Asking a friend if they would like to come with me. Checking with my partner if they are okay to watch the kids while I attend the class. Driving to the location of the class a few days before so I know where I am going. Get my yoga gear ready on the morning of my class.

Once you have your sub-goals listed out; go back through them, identifying those where you feel you may hit an obstacle. Where you find yourself asking "Yeah, but what if…."

For those, quickly think of alternative courses of action to keep you moving forward. Take a deep breath and try to brainstorm. Don't assume there is no solution. We want you to find at least one way around each potential obstacle you have identified.

For example, my partner plays squash the same night I want to attend yoga. So, I could ask them to swap nights, look for an alternative yoga class or ask a friend or family member to watch the kids.

Weigh up each alternative – you can use a simple pros and cons list - and decide which one would be the best option.

Now you have a plan with some contingency in place, it is time to put your plan into action. Limit your thinking to just the immediate task that needs to get done. Put a date /time against the first task on your list by when you commit to completing it.

Finish that and then and only then, allow yourself to think about what's next. Tick off each task as you complete it and congratulate yourself on what you have achieved.

Celebrating your successes, no matter how small is very important. When we do this, we engage the reward centre of our brain. This releases dopamine which in turn helps to keep us motivated. Also, by putting energy into the positive results we are telling our brains to take note of these successful outcomes. The more we do this the quicker our brains will think positively about the scenario.

If you need to, make changes to your plan as you go along. If something does not go exactly to plan, please, please don't despair and do not give up.

Do not put energy into negative thinking. Just see it as a learning opportunity. Take some time to think about what you could do differently to get a successful outcome. Write down any new tasks needed to support the alternative approach.

We will use this technique again in a later exercise, but for now take things one step at a time. Allow yourself to take back control, move forward and stop the spiral into overwhelm.

If you feel the urge to start cycling through a list of 'what if' scenarios, remind yourself that you have a plan and that for now you have everything covered. If this persists you can use the

It's Just Head Hoo-Ha

interruption techniques, we will cover in a later chapter to stop this type of thinking.

If you feel comfortable you can tell a friend, colleague or family member what you want to do and ask them to help keep you accountable.

Good luck!

Manage Time

In the last chapter we looked at how to create an action plan to help overcome overwhelm and stop 'what if' thinking. Creating activity plans are very effective in moving you toward simple goals. They also help you to manage your time.

We all live busy lives where we find ourselves trying to juggle our time to get through a long list of things we want to get done. The feeling of having too much to do and not enough time can result in anxious feelings or overwhelm. So, we are going to share a very simple time management technique.

You can use this for your personal life or in relation to work or combine the two. If you decide to use it to manage your workload it can be useful when trying to manage your boss' expectations on how much work you can take on and when you can deliver.

You are going to plan out all the activities you want to get done during a given timeframe. Decide what you want to make the plan for – work, your personal life or combination of the two. For this exercise we suggest just looking at one week.

Using the workbook or your own paper, make a list of all the activities you want to complete.

It's Just Head Hoo-Ha

Put absolutely everything down, including breaks for lunch & dinner, picking up children, groceries, dry cleaning, exercise classes, dropping in on an elderly relative - anything that involves your time. Make this list comprehensive, leave nothing out.

Go through and put an estimated time to complete the task. Don't worry about being too accurate, just give it your best guess.

Go through your list again and see if there are any activities you can combine to save yourself time.

Now decide which activities you will do day by day. Write the day next to each task. Once you have them listed day by day count the total number of hours you would need to complete everything on each day.

Ask yourself whether you have enough time each day to get everything done. If yes, great! You can feel calm and in control of your schedule.

If you have days with more activities than you have time for you need to prioritise. This is an approach adapted from the Eisenhower Matrix.

First, put the number 1 against all the activities that you absolutely must do that day. These are the non-negotiables. Put a 2 against the activities that you need to complete but, if necessary, could be shuffled to another day. Put a 3 against anything you could ask somebody else to do for you and put a 4 against anything that does not have to get done and is not important to you. These are the activities that you can stop doing. If you have ended up with nothing in the number 4 bucket, take another look at your list. There will be something on there that you can drop.

This method will help you to prioritise your time. You can now see what needs to get done and how much time you realistically have available in your day. When you plan your time in this way, it allows you to see you have more time than you realise, and it cuts out the overwhelm. If you found this approach useful add it to your strategy document.

Often busy people don't realise just how much they achieve. This exercise can give you a renewed respect for yourself. We tend to focus on the 'extra' tasks we would like to get done or worse still on what we didn't manage to achieve and completely ignore those regular essential chores because they are what we always do. Therefore if, at the end of the day or week, we don't achieve those extra tasks, we can end up feeling annoyed or frustrated, adding fuel to our negative view of ourselves.

Most likely you have achieved a great deal and only missed a few lower priority tasks. Writing this type of detailed plan can help you celebrate the amount you DO achieve rather than beating yourself up about what you don't get done.

We would like you take just a few moments at the end of each day and think about ALL the things you have done. Writing these things down before you go to sleep will be the fastest way for you to build self-esteem and a sense of achievement. In our society as soon as we achieve something, we focus on what's next!

Don't get tangled up in judging how well activities went, just make a list of what you got done.

It's Just Head Hoo-Ha

Interruption Techniques

In this Chapter we want to look at how you can stop spiralling into panic and repetitive anxious or negative thoughts. To stop as soon as you start to feel anxious or to stop your mind from going over the same thoughts again and again. We will explore different Interruption techniques for you to try. These are techniques you can employ to help to break your pattern of thinking when anxious thoughts are on a repetitive loop in your head or when you feel anxious feelings are starting to rise. You can use these to over-ride what has become your automatic response by engaging your pre-frontal cortex, the decision-making part of the brain, to take back control and divert your thinking.

The more you can stop the thoughts from taking hold, the less they will present themselves over time. Our brains are always looking for repeated patterns and so if your brain gets no emotional response when your anxiety is triggered, the trigger itself will gradually fade away.

The techniques are very simple. Their very simplicity may lead you to want to dismiss their effectiveness. We ask you to trust us on this one. As well as interrupting your thought pattern, the simplicity and ordinariness of the techniques create a juxtaposition and so helps to calm what can feel like very big feelings or responses. Our approach here is about taking small, easy to achieve steps that move you into the place you want to be.

First up is what we call **ten fingers**. When you first start to feel anxious, acknowledge the feeling: "Okay, I feel jittery, my heart is racing, my palms are getting sweaty" or whatever is the tell-tale sign for you. Take a deep, purposeful breath in and release it. Then start to list what you can notice around you. Physically use your fingers to count them off. Let's say you were on a train:

One: I can feel the air conditioning on my face

Two: The man opposite has a nice brown satchel. That would make a nice present for Uncle Bob

Three: The windows really need cleaning.

Four: Wow! That lady is really engrossed in what's on her phone.

Five: There are five people wearing blue coats. Imagine if they were wearing orange instead?

Six: The poster above my head has 23 words written on it

Seven: There are ten lights in each section of the carriage

Eight: Nobody is holding a coffee cup

And so on, up to ten. You can be as inventive and as silly as you like. In fact, if you can inject a bit humour into your ten things that's great, as laughter will help to cut through how you are feeling.

It's important to focus on things you like or find pleasing; you are looking for little moments of joy. Even without humour consciously diverting your attention to something else helps you to calm down. If you find your thoughts drift away from your ten things, just start from where you left off.

Take a few deep breaths in and out, bringing your shoulders away from your ears. Allow this simple action to represent calm to you.

It's Just Head Hoo-Ha

Next is a very simple interruption technique. Again, you need to acknowledge the anxious feelings and then say to yourself: "**No thank you, I'm fine**". Be sure to say it calmly and slowly in your head – or even out loud if you are on your own.

Imagine pushing the thoughts away or putting your hand up to block them. Divert your attention to something else. Focus in on your surroundings. It sounds very simple, which it is, the key is to interrupt the pattern of thinking. Rather than allowing the thoughts and feelings to build you are essentially saying "Stop!". It may take multiple attempts to halt the anxious feelings but know that they will pass. Do not give in to them. Keep repeating "No thank you, I'm fine" slowly and calmly and following up with a diverting thought.

The more you use this technique the quicker your brain will start to respond. Our brains are innately lazy and are always looking for repetitive behaviour, so if you persist with stopping your anxious thoughts this way, your brain will get the idea and stop bothering you with them.

And the last is **singing**. Yes! You read that correctly. Of course, it may not always be possible to burst into song, but when you have the opportunity, this is a lovely way to interrupt anxious or negative thoughts from taking hold. If you are not able to sing out loud you can either hum to yourself or sing the words in your head. Again, this is a diversionary technique to give you the space to restore calm.

Singing is very consuming – not only do we have to think about the words we want to sing, the timing and the music, but also the breathing. We breathe much deeper when we sing which will help calm everything down for you. Research by the British Academy of Sound therapy has shown that singing has positive effects on our mental and physical wellbeing.

When we sing for pleasure our cortisol (stress hormone) levels lower. Certain songs release dopamine (the pleasure hormone) and if combined with dancing, release endorphins (the feel-good hormones). Not only this but the study shows that our immunoglobulin A, an important immune boosting anti-body, levels increase.

We recommend having a sing-along at home or in the car, whenever you can, to experience all these great benefits but also to get used to associating feeling good with music and song. That way when you need to call on this technique, as soon as you make the decision to start singing, whether that's out loud or in your head, your brain will make that connection to happy feelings, diverting you away from your anxious thoughts.

As well as trying these techniques also, think of other ideas for quickly diverting your attention. The key is to plan upfront which technique you are going to use.

One last thing before we close this chapter, have a think about your environment. Your environment is everything around you! From the food you eat, the books or social media posts you read to the music you listen to. If you are steeped in a toxic environment of awful news stories, bad food, and sad pop songs, you will find it so much harder to lift yourself up. So, take some time to look at what you are surrounding yourself with. Are there certain things you could stop or switch up?

Make a note on your strategy document which of these techniques you will use when you need to. In the next chapter we will share one more interruption technique called diaphragmatic breathing.

Diaphragmatic Breathing

A final strategy to practice is diaphragmatic breathing. When you feel panic start to rise, when you feel stressed or tense, or negative thoughts continue to spiral you can use this technique to quickly start to feel calmer and in control again.

Diaphragmatic breathing is simply taking a deep slow, steady breath in through the nose and taking twice as long to slowly release the breath through the mouth.

This process immediately acts as a trigger in the brain to tell your muscles to relax. By you taking control and consciously slowing your breathing down your brain will fire messages to stop the arousal of the sympathetic nervous system – which is what is responsible for the panic response.

Most of us take five breaths per minute, depending on our lung capacity, but when we feel panic rising our breathing can become rapid and shallow; it can become irregular; we may hold our breath when we inhale, and we may become short of breath. This can escalate, and we begin to hyperventilate. Deep, slow and steady breathing immediately changes your physiology and calms everything down.

While breathing is something we do every second of every day, diaphragmatic breathing will take some practice. One, to feel comfortable with the technique and two, to know what to do if a panic attack starts. You want to be able to call on this technique quickly.

You may find yourself wanting to resist using this technique, particularly in public, but be assured this is a great self-calming technique as no one notices you doing it - If you do feel panic rising and you are surrounded by others, rather than leave the situation, pull back from it in your head. Picture 'your safe place' in your mind's eye. Remember the snapshot you created during our visualisation session. Allow yourself to feel the same calmness you felt then. Breathe and relax.

We suggest practising throughout the course of your day. Whenever you have a spare moment take 4 or 5 of these deep breaths in and out and picture your safe place. Over time you will find you are able to use this breathing technique very discreetly.

Also, build this into your bedtime routine. So, just before bed, practice your breathing and returning to your safe place. Start with doing this for just 1 to 2 minutes and slowly build this up to 10 minutes. There's no rush to get to 10 minutes just take your time. You may find your thoughts start to wander, that's fine. When you notice this happening, acknowledge the thought and then bring your attention back to the sound of your breathing. The breathing exercises are a lovely thing to do just before bed regardless of whether you experience panic attacks. They help your muscles and mind to relax in preparation for a restful sleep.

We recommend listening to the recording on our website https://direction.academy/prism where we guide you through how to do diaphragmatic breathing, rather than reading the steps below. The recording will allow you to follow along and fully immerse yourself in the process. If this is not possible, read through the steps below and then try them for yourself.

A diaphragmatic breathing exercise.

Sit or lie down. Get comfortable. Close your eyes and put one hand on your belly where your belly button is. Take a deep breath in through your nose. As you do feel your belly gently expand. Bring your breath right down here.

Slowly release the breath through your mouth. Breathe in for the count of four and out for the count of eight. Do not hold your breath. If you are unable to breath in or out for this long, do what is available to you, just making sure your 'out breath' is slow and longer than your 'in breath'.

Repeat breathing in and slowly out for at least two minutes. With every breath in feel yourself fill with calmness and with every out breath feel any tension or stress leave your body. Feeling a little more relaxed with every breath. Allow everything to slow down, your thoughts, your breathing, your body. You can say to yourself 'I feel relaxed and calm' each time you breathe in.

Self-Validation and Approval

We have explored some diversion techniques you can use at the onset of anxious or repetitive negative thoughts. We are now going to look at what we consider to be some widely held disempowering self-beliefs that can have a significant influence over how we feel about ourselves.

We are going to share the importance of self-approval and validation.

We are continually faced with ambiguity in our lives by things constantly changing. Whatever new thing we are presented with, until it becomes familiar, we experience a degree of ambiguity. It is a natural human response to be uncertain and this is typically one of the times when we turn to other people for reassurance that everything is okay. Similarly, each one of us wants to be liked and accepted. Here again, this is when we seek input from others to tell us we are good people.

But it is vitally important to validate yourself. To trust yourself to make sense of the changes you are presented with, to believe in your own judgements and to like yourself.

It's Just Head Hoo-Ha

The issue with seeking reassurance from others is that invariably we do not get the reassurance we seek. Instead, it leaves us in a vulnerable position, where we are reliant on others. Everybody is wrapped up in their own individual drama. This includes our partners, our parents, our children, friends and other family members, all of whom we typically hold false expectations of. Not getting the response we want can make us feel insecure, anxious, disappointed, upset, angry, betrayed or isolated. And all because we gave the power to somebody else, somebody who was probably completely unaware they had it.

Generally, when we ask somebody else, they are responding from their view of the world which may not align with ours. There are, of course, times when we need the specific skill or expertise of a professional, such as a Lawyer or Doctor, but if day to day you are seeking reassurance from others rather than trusting yourself, you are telling yourself that they know better than you do. Over time this can lead to low self-esteem and low self-confidence.

Low self-esteem and low self-confidence can lead us to do things we do not really want to, that are inconvenient or deny us the time to do what we truly want to do. Likewise, we can find ourselves saying things we don't mean or agreeing with opinions we do not hold, just to 'fit in'.

Over time, this denial of our true self can lead to frustration, further undermine our self-confidence, cause us to unduly worry and feel anxious about trying new things or about others' opinions. It can lead to resentment and even self-loathing.

As part of your journey to reassure and validate yourself, it is important to learn to feel good about yourself without the need for others to tell or show you. By giving yourself approval and validation, you are not reliant on or at the mercy of other people. You stay more in control of how you feel and respond.

As you step out of this behaviour, you will begin to identify when you are allowing yourself to look to others, why you do it and the people who are holding you in a pattern that does not serve you well.

This is a huge shift in your energy and ownership of life. It is something to get excited about and not to fear. Know that as you step away from unsupportive people, loving and respectful people will come forward into your life. There is no such thing as a vacuum – as one energetic thing leaves, it is always replaced by another.

So, in this chapter we are going to look at some of the techniques you can employ to overcome this pattern of behaviour.

Firstly, let's look at how to deal with other people's opinions. Everybody has an opinion, and it is important to remember that other people's opinions are their own. They are entitled to their opinion but equally, you are entitled to yours. It is vital that you express your honest opinion during interactions with others rather than siding with what they say, being non-committal and not sharing your viewpoint or changing what you originally put forward simply to agree with their views.

We are not suggesting going into battle over any and everything anybody says, and we understand that this can feel daunting, so start small, choose things you feel most strongly about to push back on.

Sometimes honesty is the hardest thing. Think of how often you tell little lies in your day… we all do it, and most fly under the radar.

"You look great!" (Your friend has not been taking care of herself and looks drawn and tired, but it would be unkind and unhelpful to point that out).

Your partner is planning another Saturday with their mates, you say: "That's okay" (This is very far from okay. You want them to make you a priority, but you don't want to sound needy).

"Of course, I'll help out" (You are on your knees. You need a rest, but you don't want to not feel needed by this person).

It's Just Head Hoo-Ha

So, we would like you to write down two or three scenarios in your workbook where you found yourself not giving your opinion, giving a false opinion, or changing what you said to 'fit in'. Go ahead and write whatever comes to mind.

Now you can see this is happening for you, you need to find ways to express who are in a way that feels comfortable to you. There are gentle, non-confrontational ways you can say what you think like "I hear what you are saying, however, I think/believe …." Or "That's an interesting point of view, however I …."

Thinking about the scenarios you wrote down, have a go at framing some responses using one of the above suggestions.

We would also like you to write down some 'come backs' of your own, responses you would feel happy to use. Avoid prefixing your sentences with an apology like "I am sorry, but…" as this is giving away your power. Likewise, don't be too aggressive, using outright confrontational language like "That's not right…" or "I completely disagree…." It's about striking a balance and using words that allow you to have a voice and be true to yourself.

The one thing you don't want to do here is make up a lie. It will be tempting but it is best avoided.

Slowly start introducing the sentences you have crafted to test them out. Go gently and at your own pace. We almost guarantee there won't be any friction or cross words when you choose to use them. Remember you are not being impolite; you are making a choice for you. The more you do it, the more it becomes second nature, and you find your confidence grows, rather than rolling over or people pleasing. This can be very empowering.

The technique we have just shared works if you have the chance to respond in the moment but if you find yourself in a situation where you have had someone's opinion laid on you without an opportunity to voice your view or where there has been an unresolved disagreement you need to handle this differently. You need to remind yourself that the other person merely voiced their opinion. You do not need to take their opinion on board. You have the choice to acknowledge what they have said and then let it go. And this is key…

You have the choice.

In these scenarios say to yourself "That is their opinion. I choose to let it go" and then let it go. Do not continue to dwell on it.

It is important to recognize that during every conversation with someone else, opinions are being voiced back and forth. Some are more overt and obvious, whereas others are not so easy to pick up on and these can be the ones that we hold on to and allow to negatively impact us.

Let's say for example you are planning your summer holiday to a certain country and share your plans with a friend. They then ask you a barrage of questions like "Won't it be really hot?", "Will your apartment be air conditioned?", "Is it a long flight?" and so on. They are not giving a direct opinion, but you can infer that they don't agree with your holiday choice. In these scenarios, we can find ourselves listening to the negative chatter they have put in our heads and allow it to influence us.

Again, say to yourself "That is their opinion. I choose to let it go" and then let it go. Do not continue to dwell on it. If you find thoughts around the situation persist use a release statement to let go of the feelings associated with it and then invite how you do want to feel. For example:

"I release feeling angry and upset by what my colleague said to me about the report I wrote. I know that is just their opinion. I let this go now."

"I know I did a good job. I am comfortable with that."

We would like you write down a scenario that has happened to you where you have taken onboard what somebody else has said and allowed it to negatively impact you.

Now create a release statement to let this go.

It's Just Head Hoo-Ha

"I release x,y,z (The negative bit). I Let this go. I feel a,b,c (the good feelings you want to invite)."

Again, the more you practice letting go of other people's opinions and not taking them onboard the more this will become your default way of responding.

A common scenario for many of us is not upholding our boundaries and therefore not being able to say 'no' to other people. This can come from a fear of rejection or fear of missing out. That somehow by not doing what other people want you to do, they won't like you anymore or will stop inviting you to do things.

You can find yourself doing things you don't want to do or to try to squeeze too many things into one day. The erosion of personal boundaries is usually a gradual process. We give away a little bit more and a little bit more until we find we have lost ourselves. It can lead to undue stress or resentment, creating conflict in other relationships, feeling uncomfortable or anxious around certain people.

Saying 'no' can feel scary and very uncomfortable. We have been brought up to believe that we should help other people and always be polite, which is why so many of us struggle with upholding our boundaries. It is important to acknowledge that saying 'no' or gently pushing back does not make you a bad person. It does not mean you are selfish, rude or unhelpful. It simply means you value yourself and you value your time.

So, we are going to explore ways you can get comfortable with asserting your boundaries.

There six types of boundaries: Material things - your possessions, your home, your car and of course, money. Physical boundaries - your body, your privacy and your physical environment. Mental boundaries - your thoughts, beliefs and core values. Emotional boundaries – respecting your emotions. Sexual boundaries – what you are comfortable with sexually and time boundaries – valuing and respecting your time.

We all have each of these boundaries tested at some point as we move through life. This is a natural part of how we interact with each other. It is a lot easier to say 'no' to someone if you have already told them what your boundaries are upfront.

Let's take a workplace example, if you always agree to do overtime and cover other people's shifts for them, unfortunately, you will always be the person who gets asked to it.

However, if you let your colleagues know, for example, that you are not prepared to work weekends, as this is when you spend time with your family, if they then ask you to do so, you can remind them that weekends are for your family, and you cannot work. It feels a lot easier to push back.

Have a think about the different types of boundaries and a situation where you would like to put some boundaries in place. It could be in relation to anything – friends or family regularly coming over unannounced, your work/life balance, lending things or money to other people, running errands, anything.

Boundary setting feels more comfortable when you can offer an alternative. So, in the example of friends or family regularly coming over unannounced, the conversation could go something like "It's always lovely to see you, but I would appreciate if you could give a quick call before coming over".

Don't be tempted to apologize or over-explain as that's when you can tangle yourself up and start to feel uncomfortable. Keep it short and to the point. The chances are the other person does not even realise what they are doing and the impact it may be having on you and will be more than happy to respect your boundaries.

Not all scenarios will allow you to set boundaries but for the most part you know the types of interactions where you really want to be saying 'no', based on previous experiences. For these, preparing what you are going to say in advance is helpful. It stops you from panicking and just caving in.

It's Just Head Hoo-Ha

So, we would like you to think of either a past or an upcoming scenario where you would have liked to say 'no'. Write down what you would say to the person asking something of you.

For example: "No, I cannot take your children to their training class this evening. I have a busy evening."

Remember don't fall into the trap of giving a lengthy explanation that is peppered with apologies or compromises. Keep your response short and to the point. Also, don't be tempted to lie, even if it is a white lie as these always have a way of being uncovered.

If it is a scenario where your reason for 'no' is simply that you don't want to do it you can say "No, that's not my thing" or "No, I want to catch up on (whatever it is you plan to do instead)" and leave it at that.

The more you are tempted into justifying your position the more uncomfortable you are likely to feel. You can try giving your response and then counting to 10 in your head to fill the gap in case there is a lull in the conversation. If the other person tries to cajole you into changing your mind, simply repeat your response.

If you find yourself in a scenario where you are unsure whether you want to do what is being asked you can say: "Can I come back to you?" This gives you the space to think it through and if you decide not to go ahead, to prepare your response.

It is harder to change an existing dynamic rather than setting the ground rules from the outset. The most testing boundaries are around your family, whether it's with your partner, parents or own children. These are the most difficult to navigate, as they are the most emotionally charged.

Let's start with your children – if you have them. It takes consistency and determination to uphold boundaries here as kids seem to innately know your trigger points and play on that strong desire within you to nurture and to be liked. You can find yourself 'letting them off' because you do not want to upset them or to feel they do not like you.

It's all too easy to get drawn into these feelings so it is helpful to step back from the emotion of the situation and look at what it is you are really trying to do by asserting a particular boundary. If you look at the situation objectively, most likely you will find what motivates you will be a desire to teach them respect or appreciation; how to behave in relationships, a life skill or some other important life lesson; In which case you can trust your motivation is good and that the boundary is worth upholding.
In any given scenario you can take a moment and ask yourself:

'If I let this go will this support them longer term?'

'Will this help them build a useful set of life skills?'

'Will this make them a kinder, more understanding person?'

'Are they going to be able to look after themselves and their homes when the time comes?'

'Will they take responsibility for themselves and own their actions?'

'Will this help them build loving and respectful relationships?'

'Will this help them build resilience?'

If at any point your answer is 'probably not', then you can give yourself the permission to uphold your boundaries and reframe the situation.

In the long run - and let's face it parenting is a marathon not a sprint - your kids will have more respect for you. They will learn a valuable lesson. They will have more resilience and the ability to care for themselves in the future. They will forge deeper relationships as they have been shown how to respect others. There is no downside in this scenario.

Let us now look at our relationship with our parents. These can be very difficult to navigate. Even when there is no discord between you and your parents, typically the boundary lines are very blurred. It can feel very difficult to assert them as doing so can trigger worries about not being a good son/daughter, parental disapproval or judgment, fear of abandonment.

Our parents, and/or grandparents play a significant role in creating our belief system and the lens through which we see the world. During our early life they tell us what is right and wrong, what to do, how to dress, what traditions to follow – everything about how to be in the world. This is the expected role of parents during our formative years.

Unfortunately, all too often parents continue in this role even once we become adults. As we discussed earlier in the book, we are all creatures of habit. Our brain learns certain patterns of behaviour that it then repeats. Parenting is no different. Your parents learnt to be your guide when you were too young to do this for yourself, these patterns of behaviour became the default way you interact with each other. The issue is when parents do not learn how to stop acting this way. What started as a very necessary part of your upbringing morphed into interfering or disempowering behaviour as you became an adult. Most likely, your parents are not doing anything different to what they did when you were a child, and they got the reward of seeing you blossom and grow into the amazing person you are today. However, as an adult, with your own frame of reference, your own desires, ideas and beliefs, you need the space to express yourself freely and independently. This is very important for your self-confidence and self-belief.

There are broadly two scenarios that can play out with our parents. The first is where parents stand in judgment of their children; sharing unsolicited opinions on their life choices, acting as though whatever their children do is not good enough or expecting them to still be at their beck and call. This kind of behaviour holds you in a submissive role, where you are continually trying to please them. When the brutal truth is you will never 'please' them as no sooner do you do one thing, they come back with something new. No surprise that this will chip away at your self-confidence and self-worth.

In this scenario, decide when you will make time for Mum and/or Dad and let them know. This then becomes the time you dedicate your energy to them, whether that is giving them a call, visiting them, doing jobs for them or running errands. This approach is not going to change their behaviour toward you, but it allows you to feel more in control rather than their energy seeping into your day-to-day life.

The other scenario is where parents continue to 'do' for you. This is a tricky one to recognise, as it is lovely when parents want to help out their kids, but there is a tipping point where it becomes unhelpful. If parents are allowed to be too involved in your adult life, it can strip away some of your authority and therefore undermine your self-confidence. Doing things like your washing, coming over to do the garden for you, always being the ones to organise family get togethers, which on the face of it seem kind and helpful, can make you feel incapable, inadequate or undermined.

We are not saying for one moment that Mum or Dad is deliberately trying to sabotage your life and, in both scenarios, most likely they are doing what they believe to be the 'right thing' or following how they experienced their parents. However, if it feels like your parents are the ones in control of your life, even just one aspect of your life, then it is time to assert your boundaries. You need to feel in control, to feel capable.

You can let them know that you are going to take back whatever job it is they are doing for you. You may decide on a compromise where you allow them to do certain things while you take control of others, but you must decide what you find acceptable. Simply explaining 'I feel I need to do x for myself' or 'I would like to try to do y' should be enough.

Of course, we have described two extremes, whereas your relationship with Mum and/or Dad may be a more watered-down version; nevertheless, we recommend having a think about the dynamic between you and where it would be good to assert your boundaries. A good measure of where you need to focus is how you feel after an interaction with them. If you come away feeling put down, shamed, frustrated, humiliated, angry, undermined, stupid, disrespected, unheard or like a child, then it is time to do something about it.

It's Just Head Hoo-Ha

Ask yourself what you would consider reasonable in terms of the demands and expectations they put on you. What level of contact with your parents would allow you to feel like a good son or daughter? And what is too much? Seek to introduce boundaries to support this.

And lastly partners. Again, a very complex area, where all kinds of emotions can be triggered. Fear of not being liked or loved, fear of being abandoned and fear of not being good enough being the big-ticket items. All of these can fly under the radar and rarely manifest as conscious thought, but these will be what lurk behind the reason why you act the way you do with your partner, and likewise why they behave the way they do.

Let's look at just a few examples of how this can play out in your relationship. Putting up with bad behaviour.

This relates to all manner of things, like putting up with belching at the dinner table, never challenging why your partner is always late or does not think to tell you where they are when you are expecting them to be home or leaving dirty clothes on the bathroom floor. To push back on behaviour like this can feel scary and you may feel you run the risk of losing your partner if you do.

Taking on most of the household chores even if you are both working, whether that is paid work or childcare also tells a story. This often stems from the fear that somehow you are not good enough so if you take on all the housework, shopping, errands and do everything for everyone, you will earn your place. Or similarly, if you dare to push back your partner won't like it, so won't like you, because you can't quite believe they would love you for you and ultimately, will leave you.

Always agreeing to do what your partner wants, not taking time for yourself or doing things you don't want to do often are again tell-tale signs of misplaced lack of self-worth. As if your opinions and desires do not count or are not worthy of consideration.

If you resonated with any of these scenarios there is a high chance you told yourself 'But I don't mind. It's not that big a deal' as you read on. There may be some truth in that, as all relationships require a degree of compromise and of course, you need to be careful you are not railing against everything your partner does, but equally you need to be honest with yourself. Otherwise, you are not honouring yourself and ultimately, are undermining your self-worth. You deserve to be free to express your opinions, wants and needs. You have value.

Have a think about your relationship with your partner, or how you behaved in previous relationships if you do not currently have a partner. Were there certain things you allowed that perhaps you could have gently pushed back against?

If you decide to discuss any of this with your partner, be sure to not be confrontational. It is unlikely they are behaving a certain way to deliberately hold you back or to undermine you. These are just the roles you fell into. Share how you feel and ask them for their ideas on how to change things up a little. Discuss rather than accuse. It is easy for the emotions you have been repressing to bubble up into anger and to then direct that anger at the person you see as causing the situation. To avoid this happening, use the current story technique to explore what is happening and how you feel about it. Then use the replacement story to decide what you would like to happen. Identify what your idea of happiness looks like. Try and do this without second guessing what you believe everyone else's needs to be. This is about you. You will find yourself compromising along the way and that's fine.

Release any negative feelings and invite how you want to feel. We recommend going through this process before deciding to talk to your partner, parents, friends or work colleagues. You will feel much more in control.

As with all these techniques, take your time. Just choose one or two situations where you are doing something you really don't want to and start there. Gradually start to use this more and more over time. Remember, if you take on too much change at once, you are likely to feel uncomfortable and overwhelmed. So, go slowly and at a pace that feels right to you.

If you experience some pushback from people, think about the archetypes. Which one are they employing? Why do they do this?

We have written this chapter with you at the receiving end. Have a think about your parenting style if you have older children. Consider your partners behaviour. Are you playing into any of the scenarios we have looked at? If so, what could you do differently to shift the relationship into a more mutually supportive and respectful space?

Perfectionism

We believe perfectionism is the least easily recognisable symptom of anxiety. It often flies under the radar being dismissed as having high standards, being ambitious or wanting to be successful. It can manifest in any aspect of life, such as your work and career, your studies, your relationships, your physical appearance, your home and garden, your fitness.

Whilst it can be a very powerful driving force, equally it can lead to crippling procrastination and an inability to take risks or try new things. Whichever way it manifests, if left unchecked, perfectionism can negatively impact your emotional and physical wellbeing. It can lead to fatigue, stress, unhappy relationships, burnout, lack of self-worth, eating disorders and depression.

At the heart of perfectionism is a deep-seated fear of not being good enough. Like most of our fears this has roots in our formative years with three main possible influences: One, overly critical parents, parents with high expectations of success for their children or a parent, who themselves are a perfectionist; Two, the competitive nature of the education system and the pressure to achieve or three, after experiencing trauma.

Perfectionism is not easy to identify in yourself, particularly if you are only mildly affected. To help you recognise whether this may apply to you we would first like you to answer the following questions to see whether any of them resonate:

Thinking about all aspects of your life...

Do you set yourself high standards, which you often struggle to achieve?

Do you regularly criticise yourself?

Do you feel like you have failed if you make a mistake?

Do you find it difficult to accept constructive criticism?

Do you find it hard to celebrate your success?

Thinking about your studies, job or career...

Do you set yourself high standards which you often struggle to achieve?

Do you regularly criticise the work you deliver?

Do you worry about the quality of your work for some time after you have submitted it?

Do you feel you are not working hard enough?

Do you find yourself frequently working longer hours than others?

Now thinking about your relationships ...

Do you find you are always trying to please your partner and make sure all their needs are met?

Do you feel you have failed if you have an argument?

Do you worry they will no longer like you and leave you if you have a disagreement?

Do you have a set of expectations of what a perfect partner should be and beat yourself up if you don't achieve them?

Do you find it difficult to let yourself off if you feel you did not meet your partner's expectations or you made a mistake?

Do you try to avoid any negativity and always keep things 'happy'?

Do you feel your relationship is hard work?

If you answered 'yes' to more than a couple of the questions in any of the three broad categories, chances are you are experiencing some degree of perfectionism. This may not necessarily be an issue for you, in which case we do not wish you to make it one by focusing unnecessary attention on it. So, the next thing we would like you to do is to ask yourself whether you feel it is causing you any stress or anxiousness. If the answer is no, skip on to the next chapter, if yes, read on.

Bringing awareness to this trait in yourself is the first step to quietening the perfectionist in you. It may mean you are driven to over perform or conversely it may mean you have a tendency to procrastinate for fear of making a mistake. You may also find that you swing between the two behaviours. When it comes to relationships, again it will most likely be manifesting as trying too hard to please your partner. Regardless, as we have mentioned many times already, this comes without judgement. Simply accept that is how things have been up until now as we are going to explore how you can release this tendency to shift your mindset.

First, we would like you to write out your current story using the same approach you used at the beginning of the book. Think about a scenario where you feel you may have ventured into the realms of perfectionism and describe this in as much detail as you can. Use the workbook in the Shift section on the website for this exercise as a guide. https://direction.academy/prism. Go ahead and get your current story down on paper.

Now you have an understanding of what is currently going on for you it is time to start to release the energy you are holding around this. We would like you to write a release statement using the thoughts and feelings you captured. Put them into the following statement:

'I release feeling/believing/thinking x, y, z' repeat this out loud three times.

For example, if you have concerns about the quality of your work, you could write something like: *'I release my constant worry about my abilities and the quality of the work I deliver. I release all criticism of myself and my work'*.

It's Just Head Hoo-Ha

Unlike the exercise earlier in the book we are going to give you the invite statement. Yes, we are being a bit bossy here, however, we have seen too many people not quite getting this right to leave it to chance. So, we would like you to say the following:

'I am good enough. I am confident and capable. I am resilient. I am loving and lovable. I trust myself. I am safe and secure'. Repeat this three times.

While we stand by the power of affirmations in helping to re-wire your thoughts, your chimp brain - the negative voice in your head that always has something discouraging to say - can be pretty persuasive. So, to help you shift your perspective and move forward more quickly we want to explore some reframing techniques with you.

As with all anxiety inducing situations the 'power' they have over you is derived from the importance your brain assigns to them. Your brain does this based on your emotional response and the amount of attention you give to it. The more heightened your response and the more you think about something the more important your brain considers it to be. The stories we tell ourselves whether consciously or subconsciously have a huge impact here. To move through this and change your experience you need to change the story you are telling yourself.

We will guide you through this. Try to be as honest with yourself as you can.

Thinking again about the perfectionist scenario you described, which type of fear most resonates with you?

Fear of failure, of making a mistake.

Fear of not being in control – this is different to fear of being out of control. It relates to not wanting to relinquish control and trust others to support you.

Fear of being abandoned / being alone.

Let us first look at fear of making a mistake or of failing. Failure is very emotive. It can stir up feelings of embarrassment, disappointment, sadness, humiliation, anger, worry, guilt or shame. Feelings we are all very keen to avoid. So it is no surprise that failure is something most of us will do just about anything to prevent. However, trying to avoid the feelings does not help you resolve them or stop the pattern repeating – often with increased intensity. We want to get you to a place where you can look at a situation you would have previously considered to be 'bad' as an opportunity to improve and grow.

The following questions and suggestions will help you gain a different perspective:

Are / were your expectations realistic? Consider whether you are asking too much of yourself, of others or of the expected result. Could you break things down into smaller, more manageable steps and still achieve what you want?

What have you learnt? Keep things positive. There is a lesson in everything, no matter how big or small. How could your experience help other people to avoid the same thing happening? This particular situation may not have worked out, but has it meant that a much bigger incident has now been avoided for other people, for example?

Do you need the expertise of someone else to help you? Do you need additional or different resources? Admitting you need some help can really take the weight off your shoulders.

It is so rarely the case that a situation is 'all or nothing'. There are nearly always second chances, contingencies or other avenues you can explore. Think about what these might be in this scenario.

Get into the habit of saying to yourself: *'I'll try x first and if that doesn't work, I'll try something else. I'm just exploring my options'*.

Whose 'voice' is in your head when you think about this? Recall what you wrote in the current story exercise. Is it really yours or does someone else come to mind? Often, we are trying

It's Just Head Hoo-Ha

to live up to someone else's expectations. Use a release statement to let this negative voice go.

What words of encouragement would you say to someone you respected if the same thing had happened to them? Take these words to create an invite statement and as the new voice in your head.

Let us now look at fear of not being in control. This relates to trust – not quite trusting others to help or support you in some way and / or not trusting yourself.

Ask yourself what not being in control means for you. Write down how you see it playing out. Take the scenario right to conclusion, describing all your thoughts and feelings at each stage. To help do this, keep asking yourself and 'then what will happen?' Notice whether your initial feelings that something bad will happen lessens as you draw to the end of your story.

It may be that just by doing this you can see how the story you were telling yourself was purely based on a misplaced feeling, rather than what may actually happen. If you find you still feel unsettled, take a step back and imagine you are talking to a friend who has shared this scenario. Write down some words of comfort or encouragement to address each of the objections or concerns your brain presented you with, as if you were supporting this close friend. Picture yourself talking to them if you can, to distract your attention from yourself. Use this technique to gain perspective and to start to re-write the story you have been telling yourself.

And lastly, let us look at fear of abandonment. During the current story exercise, we asked you to consider where you believe your perfectionism stems from. There is a high chance it is coming from your experience of either a parental relationship or some other significant relationship as a child. Write down your experience of this relationship and how this makes you feel about yourself. It is so important to bring these thoughts and feelings to the surface and allow yourself to acknowledge them. Take your time. This will be very emotional.

Now you can see how you have been viewing yourself up until now describe how you *want* to see yourself. Remember no double negatives. So, for example, include things like '*I deserve to be happy. I am a loving and lovable person. I am fun to be with. People like me. I am trustworthy. I am kind.*' Avoid sentences like 'I don't want to be alone. I am not mean. I am not boring'. If you sit with the two sets of words for a few moments, you will notice how the first set evokes very different emotions to the second. So, we want absolute positives in your statements. Add these to your daily affirmations, if they are not in there already. Give yourself a few weeks of repeating these empowering words and then (and not before!) begin to look at how you are behaving in your relationship. Consider how you could start to introduce more of what would make you happy rather than always putting your partner first. Revisit the boundaries chapter for guidance on how to do this.

We have looked at ways to reframe the story you are telling yourself, to give this even more impact we encourage you to first listen to the Timeline recording in the Release and Invite section again, but this time thinking about the self-beliefs that came up as you worked your way through this chapter. Use the recording to recall when your perfectionist tendencies started and to release the energy linked to the memories you are holding. Then visit https://direction.academy/prism to listen to the perspectives recording. In this recording we guide you on how to build your new perspective and to start to let go of some of the false beliefs and fears you have been holding.

It's Just Head Hoo-Ha

Catastrophic Thinking

In this chapter we want to home in on catastrophic thinking. This is where the outcome you imagine is exaggerated and believed to be much worse than it is or would be. Where you focus on the worst possible outcome, imagining how a situation could or has gone wrong. It can relate to something that has already happened for you or something that may happen in the future. This focus on the worse-case scenario causes a lot of undue stress and anxiety.

"I didn't do well in that exam. I am going to fail it and my life will be ruined!"

"I am going to mess up the presentation next week. We will lose the contract and then my boss will fire me".

"They didn't respond to my text; they don't like me".

Think carefully about whether this applies to you. It may not be a regular place you find yourself, however, it may be something that happens now and then, particularly during times of high uncertainty or stress.

Most people who experience catastrophic thinking would not necessarily see it in themselves and are only able to recognise it if they take a step back and dispassionately review their thoughts.

We would like you to think of a time when you assumed the worst. Write down what sparked this kind of thinking and what your thoughts were at the time. For example:

"I didn't call my friend when I said I would. I am sure they will think I don't care about them and won't want anything to do with me anymore."

Go ahead and write your experience down.

Now look at what you have just written and imagine a close friend or family member had said this to you. What would you say to them? We assume you would not agree with them but instead try to suggest an action step they could take to reassure them of a better outcome. With this in mind, re-write your story with this different perspective. For example:

"I didn't call my friend when I said I would. I will give them a call and explain what happened. I am sure they will understand."

You now have a different view of the situation. This is called reframing. Each time you find yourself having catastrophic thoughts take a moment to follow this method.

If you are someone who regularly thinks this way, it is critical to leave judgement of yourself behind. Stop beating yourself up

It's Just Head Hoo-Ha

for having these kinds of thoughts or believing that there is something wrong with you or that you are going crazy.

Remember the more energy you give to thoughts the more importance your brain will assign to them. Everybody has disturbing thoughts from time to time. Remind yourself that you are doing okay.

Start by acknowledging the thought. And say to yourself "*I am having one of those thoughts where I think xxx. I know this thought will pass.*" Next write out all the thoughts buzzing around in your head to bring full awareness to what you are thinking. Then re-write your story as you would if you were talking to a trusted friend or family member and trying to get them to see a more positive outcome.

If you find yourself in a situation where you cannot stop and write your thoughts down, do some diaphragmatic breathing while you wait for the thoughts to pass. Listen to the breathing exercise on our website https://direction.academy/prism for how to do this. But make sure to take the time to follow the steps above when you have a moment to yourself again. If you plan to use this reframing technique, note it down in your strategy document.

Taking Action

So, now you are ready to make some big, life changing, transformational shifts in your mindset. We want you to feel excited and capable. As always, we will guide you step by step. We are going to bring all the techniques we have explored so far, together.

You are going to develop a practical and effective plan to allow you to conquer your anxiety, overwhelm or negative thinking. Before we go into the detail of what you need to do, we want to give you an overview of what you will be doing so that you understand how it all fits together.

You start by listing out all the scenarios that cause you to feel disempowered and rank them by the impact they have on you. So, you may for example experience social anxiety. Therefore, you will list out all the different scenarios that trigger this for you, including both the ones that cause you a great deal of distress, as well as the smaller ones. You will choose just one of the least impactful scenarios to begin with, whilst you build your confidence and feel comfortable with the approach. So, for example, maybe going for coffee with friends is less triggering

It's Just Head Hoo-Ha

than going to a big event, like a wedding, where you don't know many people.

To get a full understanding of what is currently going on for you, you will write out your current story for that specific situation. We then look at the outcomes you want, by writing your replacement story.

Once you have full awareness of what is going on for you, you decide which coping strategies you will use when you need them, whilst confronting your chosen scenario. So, you may decide you find diaphragmatic breathing and saying to yourself: 'No thank you, I'm fine' effective, for example.

We then guide you through a visualisation that brings your replacement story to life in your imagination. To practice feeling and behaving the way you want to, rather than being at the mercy of your stress, anxiety, overwhelm or negative thinking. You tell your subconscious how you want the scenario to play out. You first take back control in your mind before doing it for real. Your brain doesn't know the difference from real and imagined thoughts when it comes to your emotional response, which is what makes this technique so powerful.

You then create a plan of small, practical steps you will take to allow you to meet your fears, panic, worries or negative thinking head on, so that you remain in control of the scenario you have chosen to address. We call on the planning technique we explored when committing to do something new and fun as part of the timeline exercise.

And then you will feel ready and able to put your plan into action. You know you have a strategy, and you know you can do this because you have chosen the strategies and the plan is yours.

Once you have decided on a plan for the first scenario, you put it into action straight away, using the various techniques you feel comfortable with. Those chosen to keep yourself calm and confident whenever that scenario arises.

In some cases, the previously triggering situation may not happen straight away, you won't be going to a wedding every week for example! In this case, park this one and simply go back to your list and pick another scenario to work on.

Keep moving forward. Celebrate every success, no matter how small. Keep a record of all your plans and scan through them regularly to remind yourself that you know what to do when each scenario does come up and equally to review how much progress you have made.

Over time you will have planned for and confronted all scenarios on your list and will find you have successfully conquered your anxiety, stress or negative self-talk.

So, let's get started.

The purpose of this next set of exercises is to bring full awareness to your anxiety or negative chatter to allow you to release the associated thoughts, feelings .and emotions and to reinforce your new way of thinking – more specifically, to believe you have the skills to handle what is going on for you and ultimately to stop the cycle. This is you finding the real deep root cause of your negative mindset.

Take a moment to think back on all the work you have already done. You are amazing. Stay strong!

We are going to dig down much deeper to expose every single anxious or negative thought, feeling and emotion to eliminate the frequency, intensity and duration.

This may feel a little overwhelming, but we ask for you to trust the process. Know that we will work at a steady pace and that we will guide you through exactly what to do every step of the way. You have done a lot of the work already.

So, we want you to either open your workbook for this exercise or use your own paper to write on as needed.

Relax and be yourself. Give yourself the time and space you need.

It's Just Head Hoo-Ha

Now take a few deep breaths in and out, bringing your breath right down into your abdomen each time. Shrug your shoulders up to your ears and then down. Gently, squeeze your shoulder blades closer together to widen across your collar bones. Repeat these three or four times. Each time feeling a little more relaxed. Smile!

Okay, let's make a start. Please write your responses as we go through this, rather than waiting until the end. You will find this a lot more manageable.

We want you to write down every situation or scenario where you experience anxiety, negative thoughts or panic. Do not leave anything off the list. Include even the smallest incidents.

Take your time now to try to write an exhaustive list. Make a note of as much as you can think of.

Go ahead and do this now.

We would now like you to rank your list in terms of intensity and duration. Ranking the ones that cause you the most discomfort with a one and the least impactful as three, with everything in between ranked as two. Don't worry about getting this ranking exactly right. We are just going to use it to identify which items for you to focus on first.

So, you should now have a list of every scenario where you experience anxiety, negative thoughts or panic with a corresponding ranking.

You are going to work through every item on your list eventually, but we want you to start with a scenario that you ranked as three first. If you ranked the scenario you selected to write about during the Prepare module as a three you use this one to start. If, however, the current story you wrote about has a higher ranking, go back and repeat the exercises in the prepare module to create your current and replacement story for your scenario.

The scenario you have chosen should be one that while still causing you issue is not as impactful as some other scenarios.

Please do not be tempted to ignore this and jump to tackling one of your big-ticket items. It is important to slowly build up your confidence and understanding of the techniques to avoid overwhelm and self-sabotage.

We urge you to stick with us. Keep going even if you feel you want to give up. We will guide you through this whole process. Trust that in a very short space of time you will experience huge shifts in your thinking, enabling you to take back control.

Okay so we are going to bring what we explored so far together into an action plan for the scenario you have selected.

First, re-read your current and replacement stories for the scenario you are using for this exercise and make sure they are as detailed as possible. The more detailed they are, the more you can be sure you have exposed every single anxious or negative thought, feeling and emotion to eliminate the frequency, intensity and duration. Pause here and add anything extra you feel needs to be included.

Now thinking about the techniques you included in your strategy document, describe in detail which ones you will use to combat the thoughts, feelings and emotions you experience in this scenario and when you will use them.

Let's say you want to work on feeling calmer about attending and talking during team meetings; you may decide to use 'Ten fingers' during team meetings, to practice diaphragmatic breathing every evening before bed so that you feel comfortable using this method if you need to.

You may decide to say to yourself "No thank you, I'm fine" every time you start to think negatively.

Start to develop a strategy that feels good to you, so you have a plan of what you can do if you feel anxious, panicky or your negative chatter starts. Take a few moments to reflect on this. It is important that you acknowledge that you now have a way to cope. You have a way for you to take back control even if your anxiety spikes or you start to feel low.

It's Just Head Hoo-Ha

Say to yourself "*I now have a plan. I know what to do if xxx happens*". Fill in the blank with a short description of your scenario.

Keep repeating this to yourself as we work through the different steps of this exercise.

Be Who You Want to Be

We are now going to look at how to confront your anxiety or negative chatter head on. A couple of important things to remember are:

1) How you want to respond to the scenario, so we will repeat your daily affirmations, in just a moment

2) Despite feeling anxious, panicky or low before - you coped, you got through it. We want you to feel strong and empowered as you go into this step of the exercise.

We are going to practice acting out the scenario you have chosen to focus on using visualisation. We do this to practice how you want to think and feel during the scenario, so that when you are there, you already know how you want to respond and can remind yourself if you need to.

This is more effective than waiting until you are in the scenario, as it is difficult to think of strategies in the moment if your amygdala is engaged and you are starting to feel anxious. The same technique is used by athletes and sports people. They use visualisation to practice taking that crucial goal kick or golf swing again and again in their mind so when they are confronted with the situation, the action is so ingrained that they can perform almost on autopilot, eliminating the negative effect of nerves.

Start this when you have time and can find a comfortable place to relax without being interrupted for at least twenty minutes. You can sit or lie down, whichever you prefer.

You will find guided visualisation on our website under the 'Release and Invite' section at https://direction.academy/prism.

Once you have the audio ready, get yourself comfortable, maybe grab a blanket to snuggle under, have a little wriggle around and then when you are ready press play.

Bringing it all Together

We guided you through acting out your scenario, using visualisation. The next step is to put yourself in a real-life scenario. You have a plan of what to do if panic, anxiety or negative thoughts start. You have also practiced how you are going to respond. Trust that this is how things are going to play out for you.

Using the time management technique, you are going to write a goal-based plan to help you execute this. There's no need to go back and re-read the chapter; we will talk you through the steps.

So first, write down again what it is you want to achieve – this is what you wrote in your replacement story. For example:

"*I want to ask for a promotion at work. I want to feel calm and relaxed about approaching my boss*".

Or "*I want to feel relaxed and calm about meeting my friends for a coffee*".

Now think about how you could break this down into smaller goals that give you limited exposure to start with and gradually build up to your goal. Take some time to brainstorm some ideas. Write down whatever pops into your head. For now, leave aside

It's Just Head Hoo-Ha

whether the idea is practical. We just want you to get some ideas going. To start to feel that you can conquer this. So, for example:

You could start by approaching your boss about something else to build your working relationship.

You could ask your boss about the new work position without indicating that you are interested (Unless you are asked outright of course!).

You could ask the person currently doing the job about the role.

You could speak to another member of the team about the role.

You could talk to Human Resources about the role.

Or to take the meeting up for a coffee example:

You could make a commitment to yourself to say 'yes', the next time your friends invite you for coffee.

You could just pop in briefly and see your friends in the café without ordering anything.

You could think about a couple of stories to share before you go so that you know you have something to talk about.

Feeling prepared will bring you a lot more confidence, so put some energy into doing the prep work. You will be so grateful you did.

Write down your own ideas. Identify where you feel you may hit an obstacle. Where you find yourself asking 'Yeah, but what if….'.

For those, quickly think of practical courses of action to keep you moving forward. Take a deep breath and try and brainstorm again. Don't assume there is no solution. Find at least one way around each potential obstacle you have identified.

For example: You want to start talking to your boss to build a working relationship, but you are worried you won't know what to talk about or how to make it happen.

So, you know your boss likes a cup of coffee around eleven. You could follow your boss into the coffee area now and then and just talk about the weather, sport or weekend activities. You could prepare a few things to say in advance.

If you feel comfortable approach a family member, friend or work colleague and ask for their support to brainstorm ideas.

Now you have plan in place it is time to put your plan into action. Put a date /time against the first action step in your list by when you commit to completing it. Make sure you commit to your start date to avoid procrastinating.

Limit your thinking to just the first commitment you have made to yourself. Finish that before thinking about what's next. It is a good idea to remind yourself what your coping strategies are, in case you need them and to continue to use visualisations to practice how you want to think, feel and behave whilst in the real-life scenario. One of the most beautiful re-framing techniques is to ask yourself: 'What if it goes well? What if I thrive? What if I have fun?'.

Go slowly with this and limit your exposure to start with. Each time you complete an exposure, celebrate your success and acknowledge how well you coped. Celebrating your successes, no matter how small is very important. When we do this, we engage the reward centre of our brain. This releases dopamine which in turn helps to keep us motivated. Also, by putting energy into the positive results we are telling our brain to take note of these successful outcomes. The more we do this, the quicker our brain will think positively about the scenario.

You may still have anxious feelings or negative chatter going on. Don't beat yourself up if that does happen. Just focus on the fact that you took control and confronted the scenario. And remember that the more you confront what's going on for you, the more comfortable you will start to feel. The important thing is to keep taking small steps forward.

Once you have confronted this scenario you need to go through and repeat these steps for all the scenarios on your list. Complete all those ranked as three first, then the twos and then finally, go for those you ranked as one. You will find that the process gets faster and easier the more you do it, and the more your confidence grows, the more your new way of thinking becomes your default.

Take your time with this process. We recommend tackling no more than one of these a week. While you are working your way through your list of scenarios, read the chapters on the **maintain** module and start to include some of the suggestions into your day-to-day routine.

Junilda Wright

Module five:

Maintain

Junilda Wright

MAINTAIN

Huge congratulations on making it through to this last module. Before we describe what's in store in Maintain, we invite you to stop for a moment to reflect on all that you have achieved. What has changed for you? What shifts have you made? No matter how big or small, be sure to celebrate them. We hope you are proud of yourself!

In this final module, we will be sharing suggestions you can easily incorporate into your lifestyle to continue to promote and maintain your wellbeing. These include gentle exercise routines, relaxation techniques, healthy eating suggestions to boost 'feel good' hormones and ideas on how to rest and revive. We encourage you to give these a go to see what you enjoy and what you want to start to include as part of your overall wellbeing plan.

While you are already seeing and feeling shifts in how you think, feel and behave - this module is about maintaining those changes to your emotional and physical wellbeing long term.

Each chapter has something that can enhance your lifestyle and promote happy and healthy emotions. Please try all the suggestions and see how you can incorporate different aspects of each of them into your daily and weekly routines.

They include guided meditations, mindfulness and breathing techniques and healthy eating guides. Pick and choose what you find most beneficial. If you try something for a few weeks and find it's not really helping you, try something else!

We don't recommend trying to include everything in one go as such a big change may be unsustainable. Try one or two things to begin with and as they become second nature and a natural part of your life, then try adding more. The content has been designed for you to repeat these sessions again and again as part of your overall wellbeing routine.

We would like to say congratulations once again for your resilience and commitment to getting this far. Continue to use affirmations daily. You may want to change the message every now and then as things evolve for you, which is fine. They are just a lovely, simple way of maintaining positive, happy thoughts as you continue forward.

While this may be the final module in the PRISM program, know that this is just the beginning of your journey as you find your levels of happiness, confidence, resilience, calm and contentment continue to grow.

We wish you love and joy.

We hope you have enjoyed the book. If you have any feedback and you haven't already shared it, please leave us a review.

It's Just Head Hoo-Ha

Mindfulness & Meditation

We are going to explore the benefits of mindfulness and meditation as tools to promote feelings of calm and contentment.

Let's first look at mindfulness. Mindfulness is about noticing what is happening in the present moment, both internally and externally. Within our body and in our surroundings – all without any judgement of 'good' or 'bad' about what is happening. Just calmly observing. It is this allowing things to just be and being in the moment that makes this technique so effective.

Anxiety by its very definition is either worrying about something that we believe may happen or something we believe has happened, so by concentrating on the here and now, you calm those worries and let them go. Using Mindfulness exercises will allow you to accept the unsettling feelings that mark the onset of a panic attack without labelling them as 'bad' and in this way, undermine their power.

They also buy you some time so that you can adjust your response. Then, rather than starting to notice your tell-tale signs of anxiety rising and spiralling into a full panic attack, you can employ a **mindfulness** technique to stay calm, focused and in control, making it easier for you to deal with the situation.

Let's do a short exercise you can start using straight away. Find a quiet space where you will not be interrupted. Sit down and get comfortable. This is an exercise Margaret Wehrenberg shared in her book "The 10 best-ever anxiety management techniques".

If you would prefer to listen to us guiding, you through this technique visit our website at https://direction.academy/prism.

Relax your shoulders, take a nice deep breath in and out. Take another lovely deep breath in through your nose. Notice how the air feels as it fills your nostrils, the coolness of the air. How it feels as it goes down the back of throat and starts to fill your lungs. Notice the feeling as your ribcage expands, as your diaphragm expands.

Exhale and notice how the breath feels as your lungs deflate, as the air travels back up through your throat and out through either your mouth or nose. Feel the warmth of the breath. Notice how your clothes feel. Notice the feel of the chair you are sitting on.

Great. Now as you exhale turn your attention to your surroundings. Notice what you can hear, what can you smell, what can you feel. Is there any movement near you?

Switch your awareness back to your breathing. Breathe in and again notice the coolness of the breath. The sensation in your nose and throat. How your lungs expand.

Now, exhale and notice the reversed sensations as your lungs empty of air, up into your throat and either mouth or nose. Notice how your clothes feel and the chair underneath you.

Exhale and bring your focus back to where you are. Again, what you can hear, what can you smell, what can you feel. Is there any movement near you? Has anything changed since you last focused here?

It's Just Head Hoo-Ha

Once more take a lovely deep breath in. Feel your nostrils fill with air. Down the back of your throat and down as your lungs expand.

And breathe out. Your ribcage becomes smaller. Notice your breath travelling up and out. Warmer air. Notice how your clothes are feeling. How the chair beneath you feels.

Exhale and shift your attention once more to your surroundings. Listen. What can you hear? What can you smell? What can you feel? Is there any movement?

Notice the light and the colours all around you. Stay here for a moment and when you feel ready continue with your day.

We recommend practising this technique at home to get used to what you need to do and then you can use it when you need to whilst out and about. The 'ten fingers' technique works in a similar way, drawing your attention to what is immediately around you and focussing on the here and now.

If you find yourself in a situation where anxious or negative feelings are closing in, we encourage you not to leave the triggering situation but instead sit and go through this exercise. It will help you to feel calmer and more at peace in the situation.

If this is a technique, you feel you want to use as part of your action plan. Write it down so that you can refer to it if you need to.

There are lots of great apps and videos on Mindfulness available so you can explore other exercises.

Meditation is another technique that is proven to promote feelings of calm and contentment. We can understand that the very mention of the word meditation may have you wanting to run for the hills, but we ask you to stick with us and be open to exploring this deeply relaxing approach.

There has been lots of research around the benefits of meditation. It has been proven to help to reduce anxiety – which of course is why we are looking at it, but also to reduce stress, by reducing cortisol levels (the stress hormone), promote 'good' feelings and increase positivity, helping to combat depression and aid restful sleep. These benefits are achieved by changing the frequency of our brain waves.

During our normal day-to-day, we are typically in what is called a beta brain wave state. This allows us to experience conscious thought and logical thinking. As with everything to do with the brain, it's all about balance. So, if we experience too much it can lead to stress and anxiety as we tend to be overly stimulated. Caffeine and energy drinks can put us into this state. Conversely, too little beta may result in difficulty concentrating and in some cases depression.

When we meditate, we move to what's called an alpha brain wave state. This is the same brain frequency we are in as we move from full consciousness and transition in to sleep (which takes us into theta). This frequency is very calming and helps us to deeply relax.

Meditating for just 15 minutes a day has been shown to have a significant positive impact. A lot of people are put off meditation believing they need to completely clear their minds. But that is not what meditation is about. It is just taking some time to breathe, to slow things down and relax. To allow thoughts to drift in and out. With practice you will find your thoughts slow right down and you reach alpha state very quickly. The key is to just allow your thoughts to come and go, rather than fighting to clear your mind. Otherwise, you may find yourself feeling unsettled or frustrated that you are unable to clear your head.

We recommend combining your meditation with your diaphragmatic breathing exercises. The two go perfectly together as deep breathing is very calming. It helps you to quickly get into alpha state. Build up your routine slowly. Start with meditating and breathing for a few minutes just before going to sleep and gradually increase the time to 15 minutes over a few weeks. There is no rush. Also, don't be tempted to keep questioning whether you are doing things right or achieving alpha state. The only question to answer is: do you feel calmer and more relaxed?

It's Just Head Hoo-Ha

We would like to show you just how simple and deeply relaxing meditation is, so head over to our website where we have recorded a short session.

Physical Exercise

We all know that regular exercise is good for our heart and lungs, our mobility, flexibility and can help control our weight. It also aids restful sleep, has a significant impact in reducing stress levels and promoting happy feelings.

Aerobic exercise, yoga, muscle relaxation and gentle stretching and movement, all have real benefits in overcoming stress and anxiety and boosting feelings of wellbeing. No matter where you are in terms of physical fitness, have a go at each type of exercise and then choose one or two to follow at least twice a week. There are plenty of videos you can access on the internet. It may take practice but stick with it. Trust that your fitness levels will improve and that each time you do an exercise you are showing your mind and body how to feel relaxed and calm.

This is an area where we often start off with great intentions, but over time stop exercising. To keep motivated you can set yourself targets to achieve each week – be sure to set realistic, achievable targets otherwise this can be de-motivating. Decide which days of the week and what time you will exercise and then stick to it so that it becomes part of your weekly routine.

Maybe find yourself an accountability partner, somebody you feel comfortable sharing your exercise goals with and who you

It's Just Head Hoo-Ha

know will give you that gentle push to keep going. Ask a friend or family member to do the exercises with you or if you can afford it, get yourself a personal trainer.

Physical tension is due to too much noradrenaline, this is what produces the feeling of alertness and feeling 'wired'. Relieving physical tension helps us to relieve emotional tension. And if you are feeling calm and less tense physically, it is harder to then spiral into panic.

Relaxing your muscles not only relieves any tightness or aching, but also helps signal to the parasympathetic nervous system to slow your heart rate and breathing down and to lower your blood pressure, all of which help you to feel calmer and more relaxed. In the same way that diaphragmatic breathing and meditation help you to achieve this, yoga, gentle stretching and muscle relaxation exercises promote the same feelings.

Aerobic physical activity helps us to use up excess adrenaline and to rid our bodies of Cortisol produced as a response to stress. Having consistently high levels of cortisol disrupts our ability to relax and sleep, may manifest as headaches and back pain, and may cause weight gain.

Aerobic exercise increases the blood flow to the brain, improving the function of the neurotransmitters. This includes an increase in serotonin levels – low serotonin has been linked to low mood.

Brisk walking and dancing are things you can fit easily into your day, they require no equipment or preparation. You can start today. Decide to leave your car and walk or park further from your place of work and walk the remainder. Pop on your favourite dance tunes whilst preparing dinner and really go for it whilst waiting for things to cook. Just twenty minutes doing one of these is an excellent way to increase your heart rate and to get the benefits described.

Take action!

Choose one or two types of exercise to try.

Take a positive view of exercise; rather than thinking of it as a chore or something you dislike doing, think of it as something enjoyable, that is fun and that boosts your mood and your energy. Something that makes you feel happy and alive.

Muscle Relaxation Technique

We want to share a technique for relaxing each muscle group.

When we are stressed, we tend to tighten up our bodies. We unconsciously tense muscles, resulting in headaches, shoulder and back pain. This is a very simple, low impact exercise you can use to release the physical tension which will then help you to relax and release any emotional tension.

This is a nice one to include in your bedtime routine instead of – or if you like – as well as a warm bath.

You can read through how to do this and then give it a go or if you would rather listen to us talk you through as you do it, head over to our website at https://direction.academy/prism to listen to the recording.

To begin, sit down and close your eyes. Start with a few deep breaths. Take a nice long and steady breath in through your nose, fill your lungs and then slowly breathe out through your mouth. In and slowly out. Take two or three slow breaths in and out.

Now imagine a safe place, somewhere you feel relaxed. Somewhere you feel the warmth of sunlight on your body. Imagine the feel of the gentle, warm light and as you breathe in, the colourful energy of this light fills your body. And as you breathe out you feel tension start to leave you.

Bring your attention to **your head**. Raise your eyebrows and feel your scalp move. Lower them. Repeat this three times.

Wrinkle your brow into a frown, breathe out to smooth out your forehead. Repeat three times.

Now squint your eyes, wrinkle your nose and purse your lips. Release as you breathe out. Repeat three times.

Give a big yawn, stretch your mouth. Breathe out to release. Yawn and release three times.

Onto your neck. Take care not to force any of the movements. If anything hurts pull back from it. This is not meant to be painful. Gently allow your head to fall forward as your chin meets your chest. Back to centre. Then tilt your head back – gently and then back to centre. Do this three times.

Tilt your head to the right bringing your right ear down to meet your right shoulder – only go as far as is comfortable. Back to the centre. Now the same on the left side. Centre. Repeat three times: right, centre, left, centre.

Shoulders now. Hunch your shoulders up to your ears. And down. Again, repeat three times.

Onto your arms. Tighten your forearm and clench your fist. Release. Repeat three times.

Moving down to your abdomen. Pull your tummy in as if pulling your belly button back towards your spine. Let go. As you breathe out, pull your tummy in and release on the inward breath. Repeat three times.

Squeeze your buttocks together and release**.** Repeat three times.

Thighs now. Tighten your thigh muscles, let go. Three times.

Down to your shins. Point your toes and feel the stretch along your shin. Relax. Repeat three times.

Calves. Flex your toes up and release. Three times.

Curl or scrunch up your toes. Let go. Curl them. Repeat three times. As you release your feet back to the floor after the third time take another breath in and release it. Feel grounded. Feel warmth, feel relaxed and at peace.

Open your eyes when you have finished and set the intention for this feeling to stay with you. Take notice of how you are feeling in this moment. Recognise that you can feel relaxed and calm. Acknowledge that you can induce this feeling when you choose to do so. You are in control.

Gratitude

It is helpful to focus on what's good in your life. We often get caught up in our day to day lives and don't take time to celebrate the small things. Similarly, we can find ourselves focusing on what's next and forget to acknowledge what we already have.

A lovely simple technique is what we call 'what three things?'. It's a daily ritual that you do first thing in the morning looking back on the previous day to set you up with some positivity for the day ahead. All you do is think of three things that you enjoyed, made you happy or made you smile. Include small items of joy that appeal to each of your senses. The touch of something, smell, taste, sound, sight. For example, a nice hot drink in the morning, the feel of a hot shower, taking the dogs for a walk in the park, watching your favourite film, the smell of fresh laundry, the sound of birds singing, squishing your hand into a bag of dried rice just because it feels nice. Talking to the check-out assistant in the supermarket. A delicious meal.

Go ahead and think of three things now. Have some fun with it. Allow the happy memories and feelings associated with what comes to mind to bubble up. Smile if it feels good. Enjoy the feelings.

It's Just Head Hoo-Ha

You may find you draw a blank at first, because you have shut this part of your brain down and like any new habit it takes time to form. So, here are some suggestions:

I woke up in a bed, I am grateful for that.
I have food to eat.
My home is warm.
My body is healthy and takes me where I need to go.
I have good friends who are there for me.

It might feel a bit silly but, if you have shelter, warmth and food, all your base needs for survival are already taken care of. That's not something we give much mind to. Everything else is a bonus on top of what we need to survive. It helps to keep your life in perspective, especially when it's easy to lose track of the basics.

Junilda Wright

The Three Rs

It is critical you give yourself permission to relax, release and rest. We call these the three Rs.

We live increasingly busy lives and often do not allow for 'down time'. We need to have time without any external stimuli, and we don't just mean sleep, but time when we are not busy doing something, with no T.V and no technology.

This precious time gives our brain the chance to make sense of our day, to process what we have learnt and to understand ourselves and other people. Without it we can become overwhelmed and anxious.

We have already talked about mindfulness and meditation which are great ways to click the 'off' switch. We are now going to share some more ways to achieve some time out.

Massage and Reiki are lovely therapies, not only do they give you space to re-balance, but they also help to relax muscles and release tension. Scientific research shows that physical contact with other people reduces stress and improves our mood. We release oxytocin, which has been labelled as the 'feel good' hormone as it does precisely that. It makes us feel good. If you can, it's a good idea to build a monthly massage or Reiki treatment into your maintenance plan as they help you feel soothed, calm and cared for.

If you cannot get to a professional massage therapist or Reiki Practitioner, you can always ask your partner, family member or a friend for a massage at home. There are plenty of videos online giving advice on how to give a massage and you can buy lovely massage oils either online or in health shops. You can re-listen to the Relax Reiki in the Prepare module. Head over to our website at https://direction.academy/prism. This one is lovely to listen to after a busy day or just before bed.

Having a warm bath helps to calm your mind down and relax muscles. Just like physical touch, a warm bath has been shown to release oxytocin. Adding a few drops of essential oil not only makes the water smell lovely, but if you use the same smell regularly helps your brain associate that particular scent to feelings of relaxation. The smell of the essential oil then acts as a trigger to cue feelings of calm and peace. This is a good one to build into your bedtime routine.

Getting a dose of at least fifteen minutes of fresh air every day helps to maintain our circadian rhythms, promoting restful sleep and helping to decrease anxious feelings. Walking in nature has documented benefits. Shinrin-Yoku in their book 'The Art and Science of Forest Bathing' describes studies that show how being around nature reduces blood pressure (which tends to be high when stressed) and helps to relieve physical and emotional tension. If the sun is shining, you have the added benefit of boosting your testosterone levels.

Give yourself some down time by taking a walk in a park during your lunch break or simply sitting in the garden. Park your car or bike a little further away from where you work or get off the bus or train one stop earlier and walk the rest of the journey. Bringing leafy plants into your home and / or office also helps with the nature effect.

Being close to water also has an impact on our wellbeing. Research has shown that the ions that naturally occur in the atmosphere in places near to water aid relaxation, so if it's possible head to the sea or a lake and breathe in the lovely fresh air.

Take some time now to think about what is possible for you to build into your schedule and how you can include at least fifteen minutes of fresh air every day.

Sleep

A good night's sleep is crucial for good health. The NHS recommends around 8 hours of sleep for adults. When we regularly experience poor or insufficient sleep, structures in the brain related to anxiety become overactive, we feel a lack in energy and find it difficult to focus. In addition, our cortisol levels rise which over prolonged periods can lead to weight gain, diabetes, heart attacks, high blood pressure, depression, osteoporosis and depressed immunity. Plus, lack of sleep increases the "hunger hormone" grehlin.

Grehlin is produced mainly by your stomach and acts on your brain's pleasure centre, making you reach for that second (or tenth) chocolate biscuit because you remember how wonderful they taste.

Getting a good eight hours sleep allows our brains to restore. Neurons shrink to allow toxins to be carried away from the brain and for new neurons to grow – restoring the critical balance of neurons and neurotransmitters needed for emotional (and physical) wellbeing. Quality sleep has also been shown to help boost testosterone levels.

The production of Melatonin – the thing that makes us feel drowsy and ready for sleep - can be disrupted due to stress and then we make it even harder to sleep well by eating late dinners, answering emails, 'surfing the net' or working late, watching the evening news about all the disaster, pain, and suffering in the world or programmes that include violence or suspense just before bed.

So, it's important to establish a bedtime routine that signals to our brain that it is time to calm down in preparation for sleep. Here are some very simple things you can do to promote restful sleep:

Avoid caffeinated or energy drinks at least a couple of hours before bed.

At least 30 minutes before you want to go to sleep, "power down" all your electronics: TV, smartphones, computers. The light of the back screen tricks us into thinking we are not sleepy.

Go to bed and get up at roughly the same time every single day of the week (give or take 30 minutes) to establish a pattern. As we described in the previous chapter, getting out in the fresh air for 15 minutes each day helps to regulate our circadian rhythms – which are responsible for regulating our body clock.

Try to get to bed before 10 pm. Ayurveda, a Hindu ancient medicinal system, talks about doshas, which are cycles of energy we experience at different times throughout our day. The dosha around 10 pm is when the body is most peaceful. If you stay awake after 10 pm the energies pick up again which helps to explain why people describe getting 'a second wind'.

Create a serene, calm haven in your bedroom. Remove all clutter, as this creates low lying stress. Choose soft, mellow and calming colours for the walls and your bed linen. Avoid having a TV in your room.

Spray a gentle scent like lavender or sandalwood essential oil mixed with water. If you use it consistently your brain will associate this scent with relaxation and sleep.

Having fresh, clean bedding can give a feeling of luxury and comfort.

We talked about the benefits of a warm bath – so this is a lovely one to include. Or even a warm shower and then pamper

It's Just Head Hoo-Ha

yourself a little with some face, hand or foot cream. Take time to massage it in

Whilst you are doing that you could do some breathing exercises to deeply relax. Or take ten to fifteen minutes to do some meditation.

Pause for a few moments to write down what bedtime routine you plan to put in place. This will help you to make it a reality rather than some loose thoughts buzzing about in your head with no real commitment behind them.

Once you have written your plan, decide what you can commit to starting today. Don't wait.

There may be things you cannot implement immediately because you need to buy something or redecorate, that's fine, just get going with what you can do and gradually add to your routine when you are able.

For those things that need more time make a note of when and how you can make them happen.

As well as preparing for sleep, it is a good idea to have a strategy of what to do if you awake during the night with anxious thoughts.

If you become aware that you are having fretful or worrisome dreams, take the decision to fully wake up. Once awake, ask yourself if there is any action that you need to take at that time? If so, get up and do it.

For those times when you cannot take immediate action, keeping a notebook by the bed so that you can write down what is on your mind is a good strategy. This allows you to release the worry and be assured that you will not forget what it is you need to do. Take a few moments to remind yourself that things will gain perspective in the morning.

If there is no specific focus for your worry and you are feeling a general sense of foreboding, turn your thoughts to a safe place. You need to have already created your safe place in advance, we will guide you through creating this place in the next chapter.

You can also listen to sleep meditations to help you drift back off to sleep. We have created one you can listen to on our website: https://direction.academy/prism.

Whatever bedtime routine you have decided upon please stick with it. It may take some time for your mind and body to get into this rhythm, but trust that you will get there. As is true for all the techniques we have shared, it's the repetition and the consistency that starts to create the shifts in your thinking and behaving.

It's Just Head Hoo-Ha

Your Safe Place

In the previous chapter we described creating a safe place. This is a place in your imagination that you can go to when you feel anxious, worried, low or generally out of balance and flow.

You are going to awaken all your senses and link them to the place we will help you create. This will strengthen the neural pathway in your brain. Each time you conjure up the image, the smell, feel or sound of this safe haven, it will act as an automatic trigger to your brain to calm things down. To allow you to feel relaxed, happy and at peace.

Before we get started, we ask that you trust yourself. Awaken your inner child who believed any and everything was possible. Suspend belief. Let go of questioning and give your imagination full rein.

You can read through the steps to creating your safe place below or you can listen to the recording on our website where we guide you through this. Visit https://direction.academy/prism.

It is best to lie down for this exercise. Close your eyes and as you do so, give yourself permission to begin to relax. Take some nice deep breaths.

Take a deep breath in through your nose. Fill your lungs and then breathe out through your mouth. Try to make the out breath twice as long as the in breath. Breathe in for four counts and breathe out for eight. Repeat this five times. Feel yourself relax. Keep breathing deeply. Gently move your head from side to side. Release any tension. Bring your shoulders gently up to your ears and then down. Release. Relax. Keep breathing. Feel any tension in your stomach go. Let it go. Relax your arms. Relax your bottom and your legs. Breathe.

We invite you to think of a place where you feel calm and relaxed, where you feel happy and safe. It can be anywhere. Inside or outside. Somewhere you have been or just somewhere you have created in your imagination.

Let's bring it to life. Start by imagining the feel of the sun or wind on your face, or something comforting on or under you. Maybe you are under a soft snuggly blanket or lying on fresh, springy grass. Imagine the smells around you – focus in on something you smell regularly.

It could be your morning coffee, your perfume or aftershave, hand cream, a favourite essential oil. Pause here for a few moments to really fill your nostrils with the smell you have chosen. Take three deep breaths and every time you breath in, imagine the smell.

Imagine the colours of the scene you are picturing. Choose one colour to focus in on. Pick a colour you love. Imagine you can see a big ball of light in this colour. Breathe here for two or three breaths. Allow the colour to fade to the background so you can see the scene you have created but somehow you are still vaguely aware of your chosen colour.

Imagine the noises you can hear – maybe birds, the sea ebbing and flowing, leaves rustling, music playing or maybe you are with other people, and you can hear them talking or laughing. Breathe deeply here and allow these noises to fill your ears.

Now bring the smell, the feel, the colour and the sounds together. Feel as though you are totally immersed in your scene. Your everyday world feels outside of this place. You feel safe and secure. You feel calm and relaxed. Smile. Take some deep breaths and strengthen these feelings.

As you breath you may notice an animal appear. Notice what type of animal it is. You may feel a connection with them.

When you feel ready, imagine stamping this image into your mind so you can access it again whenever want to. Notice how relaxed and calm you are feeling right now in this safe place.

When you are ready open your eyes. Now you have created a safe place.

You now have a number of routes back to this place that you can take whenever you want to. You can close your eyes and go. It is lovely to do this as you drift off to sleep. Whenever you smell the scent you choose – either in real life or by bringing it to mind and imagining you have it in your nostrils. And whenever you see your colour – again real or imagined. The more you engage with your safe place, the easier it will be to conjure and the deeper the feelings of security and contentment.

Food

We are going to talk about food and drink. You will most likely have heard a lot of this before. but it is worth going over it again as making small changes to what you eat and drink can boost feelings of wellbeing, as well as the bonus of maybe helping to lose a few pounds! Let's first look at what to avoid.

Added Sugar is an obvious one.

Sugar has no nutrients and eating too much can send you on a roller coaster. At the top, you get a quick burst of energy, but excess sugar means more insulin is produced to control the intake. This causes you to dip, which can give you that shaky, uncomfortable feeling. To try to reset the balance the body then craves sugar, and you can get caught in a vicious cycle.

This roller coaster effect puts your body under stress where weight gain, low energy, moodiness and poor health are almost inevitable. It is important to regulate the amount of sugar you consume. Some simple things you can do right now to reduce your sugar intake are:

Drink water! Swap sugary drinks for good old tap water or fruit/herbal teas. Avoid sweets, chocolate, and processed foods.

Overall, moderation is key. It is the added sugar in sweet, sugary snacks and drinks that you need to be aware of. Sugar that naturally occurs in foods like fruit for example, has the benefit of essential fibre and vitamins and so needs to be included in a balanced diet.

Caffeine is known to trigger the release of adrenaline, which as we have looked at previously is involved in our 'fight or flight' response, so it is no surprise that caffeine can leave you feeling jittery and may even bring on panic attacks, even in small quantities. As caffeine is known for making us feel more alert, it can make it difficult to get off to sleep. Try swapping to fruit teas, water or caffeine free equivalents. You may find that your energy levels increase.

Alcohol. Drinking alcohol is often seen as a way to relax and feel more comfortable in social situations as it can suppress our inhibitions, but these so-called benefits are short-lived.

Alcohol withdrawal can result in increased levels of anxiousness, panic attacks, vomiting, nausea, increased blood pressure and agitation, even after just a couple of glasses of wine.

Alcohol also impacts the quality of our sleep. Our bodies are busy trying to process the alcohol and flush it out of our systems, which means we are distracting it away from its normal night-time repair routine. Alcohol is dehydrating, which has been linked to an increase in Cortisol levels (a stress hormone) and has been shown to negatively impact the cognitive function of our brains.

Reliance on alcohol to get you through social situations may lead to alcohol dependency. It is best to try to avoid alcohol. However, if you do partake, be sure to moderate your drinking and be aware of the potential impact it can have on you the day after. Be mindful of how many units you drink per week and educate yourself on the effects.

Let us now look at what to include more of in your diet. You will find a worksheet that shows you which foods are rich in each of these on our website: https://direction.academy/prism.

Tryptophan is a naturally occurring amino acid that the body can convert to Serotonin. As previously discussed, Serotonin helps to boost our mood, which typically tends to be low in people experiencing anxiety or depression. It also promotes restful sleep.

Folate and B Vitamins. Research has shown that folate, B-12 and B-6 are involved in the vital production of neurotransmitters and deficiencies can therefore impact our mood, resulting in anxiety and depression.

Foods rich in Vitamin C & antioxidants help repair cells and therefore contribute to lowering anxiety. Cell renewal is essential in the production of neurotransmitters to keep the right balance of hormones.

Magnesium is again involved in regulating neurotransmitters, helping maintain and restore balance.

Foods rich in melatonin help us to rebalance our circadian rhythms. Our bodies start to release melatonin during the hours of darkness preparing us for sleep. If you have difficulty falling asleep, naturally boosting your melatonin levels may work for you.

Maintaining the right balance of Dopamine, which is linked to the reward and motivation part of our brain can help us recognise pleasure and keep us motivated to want to do those pleasurable things again. A lack of dopamine can leave us feeling low and lethargic.

So now you have an idea of how food and drink can impact your wellbeing, have a look at the food fact sheet on our website and decide how to start introducing more of these into your eating habits.

Conclusion

You now have a set of tools and techniques you can use to take back control of how you think, feel and behave.

We sincerely hope this is just the beginning of your journey into exploring how to bring greater harmony into your life. We firmly believe that as you deepen your connection with nature and build compassion and love for yourself, you can experience true and lasting happiness.

Junilda Wright

About the Author

Junilda (Jill) spent years in the corporate world as a Change Manager before deciding she wanted to support people in a more personal and meaningful way. She re-trained as a life coach and Reiki Practitioner. And as anyone in the coaching business will tell you, there is nothing more rewarding than being able to support others become a happier, more fulfilled version of themselves.

Jill is passionate about personal growth and is dedicated to guiding and empowering others to be their best selves - this is the reason why she and Jo set up Direction Academy. They call themselves 'life lifters' and that's what they seek to do through their online programmes and books – lift lives up!

Printed in Great Britain
by Amazon